THE TRUTH THAT
SETS YOU FREE

Also by Colin Urquhart

Anything You Ask
Faith for the Future
Holy Fire
In Jesus Christ
Listen and Live
My Dear Child
My Dear Son
My Father is the Gardener
Personal Victory
The Positive Kingdom
Receive Your Healing
When the Spirit Comes
Your Personal Bible

THE TRUTH THAT SETS YOU FREE

COLIN URQUHART

Hodder & Stoughton
LONDON SYDNEY AUCKLAND

Copyright © Colin Urquhart 1993

First published in Great Britain in 1993

The right of Colin Urquhart to be identified as the author of
the Work has been asserted by him in accordance with the
Copyright, Designs and Patents Act 1988.

British Library Cataloguing in Publication Data
A catalogue record for this book is available from the British Library

10 9 8 7 6 5 4 3

ISBN 0 340 59058 0

Typeset by Hewer Text Composition Services, Edinburgh
Printed and bound in Great Britain by
Cox & Wyman Ltd, Reading, Berkshire

Hodder and Stoughton Ltd
A Division of Hodder Headline PLC
338 Euston Road
London NW1 3BH

To all those whose
desire is to live
in the Truth, and
to know how they
can encourage others
by speaking the
Truth to them in love

Acknowledgments

I want to thank the many, many people who have encouraged me to write this book; those who have attended Direct Counselling courses and conferences, and whose lives have been changed radically as a result. A book can never be the same as 'live' ministry, but I trust this will convey to you the essence of the truth of Jesus Christ that will set you free; and that you will see how you are able to communicate the truth to others that they too may be liberated.

My thanks to my secretaries – Helena, who has borne the brunt of the word processing, Barbara and Samantha – and others who have helped.

My thanks also to my friends in the Middle East, especially Dr Susheela John. Most of the book was written while there for a time of ministry.

And of course I am deeply grateful to the Lord for His enabling, and for a wonderful wife who is so understanding whenever I am absorbed in writing.

To God be all the glory for whatever way He is able to use this book to minister His Truth into the lives of His beloved children.

Throughout this book I have used the pronoun 'he' as it is

important the teaching of the Truth is applied to each individual. Of course the Truth is equally applicable to every 'she'. The use of the masculine does not represent any sexist stance by the author!

The biblical quotations are from the New International Version, except where indicated. The use of bold and italic type in them is my own.

Contents

PART 3 OVERCOMING THE ENEMY

PART 4 DIRECT COUNSELLING

PART 1

THE TRUTH

1 Glorious Liberty

'It is for freedom Christ has set us free', Paul proclaims boldly. 'You were called to be free', he says. And yet many Christians do not live in personal freedom. They live more like victims than victors, victims of their past hurts or of their present problems. To suggest they are always led in triumph through Christ is met either with astonishment or unbelief.

They feel inadequate, useless, spiritual failures! Some even doubt God's love for them because they have sought to experience His love – but in vain! This failure reinforces their sense of inadequacy. They do not see how they could be used by God; and they expend considerable nervous energy trying to conceal their spiritual inadequacy from other Christians.

Perhaps counselling is the answer? After all, many others seem to need this and there are an increasing number of people ready to offer counsel.

In time even this often leads to disillusionment. It is good to have someone to talk to, someone who gives you time and takes a genuine interest in you. But there is the pain of going over past hurts, of having to relive things best forgotten. And there always seems to be another part of the puzzle to be discovered, as if you have to go deeper into yourself, or further into your past, to find the root cause of all this personal inadequacy and failure. And the benefits of such counselling seem so short-lived!

This can lead to a certain resignation: 'Perhaps I should learn to live with the problems. People will have to accept me as I am. At least it helps to talk, but will I ever really be free?' Such freedom as there is seems to disappear as new problems arise; the same old feelings of insecurity and inadequacy re-emerge. Will it ever get better? 'What is really wrong with me?'

Going deeper into yourself, or further back into your past, is diametrically the opposite to the teaching of the New Testament. No wonder such an approach to problems fails to bring true liberty. Neither does looking at yourself produce the faith that will enable you to face the difficulties which will inevitably arise in the future.

The purpose of this book is to show you how you can experience the freedom of which the scriptures speak: 'the glorious liberty of the sons of God'. In New Testament times Christians were so famous for the freedom they enjoyed, Paul suggests that others would want to send spies among them to see why they enjoyed such liberty.

People were genuinely set free by the power of the Gospel; so much so that they needed to be taught how to use, and not abuse, that freedom.

People only resort to unbiblical kinds of ministry, either because they do not know the Truth of what God has done for them in Jesus, or they do not understand these truths. And so they cannot believe what Jesus has accomplished for them. If their knowledge, understanding and faith are limited, they can only experience a limited freedom.

You never have to justify the Truth. If you have to justify the ministry you either exercise or receive, something seriously is wrong. Many involved in so-called 'inner healing' are trying to justify their approach from scripture, with zeal but no convincing arguments! The reason for this is simple. Methods will not rescue people from their bondages; but the Truth will.

Jesus affirms that it is the Truth itself that will set us free.

Therefore we need to know and understand the Truth of what God has done for us through Him; for when we believe the Truth it impacts our lives in the way God intends. Then we can enjoy 'the glorious liberty' He desires for His children, the freedom He has made possible through faith in Jesus.

Does God want us to be healed? Undoubtedly! Does He want to free us from the hurts of the past and the emotional inadequacy of the present? Without question!

However, these objectives will not be achieved by looking into yourself, or back into your past. They can only be achieved by taking hold of the Truth and making that Truth your own. This book will encourage you in doing just that.

I have led a number of conferences under the title, 'Direct Counselling'. These have been directed at those involved in pastoral and counselling ministries. It would be no exaggeration to say that these conferences have brought about major changes in the lives of those attending. By the end of these conferences it was as if I was speaking to an entirely different group of people from those who arrived at the beginning.

I do not claim the credit for this, for I have only used the time available to share the Truth with them; and this has had the liberating effect on them that Jesus promised.

Many write subsequently to share how their ministries to others have been revolutionised. People who have received 'counselling' for years are set free at last!

To give one example: A minister came on one conference and the Truth impacted his life and ministry to such an extent he sent his wife on a subsequent conference. He later wrote to thank me for sending back his 'new' wife and commented how people were now being set free through her ministry with astonishing speed.

That is the effect of the Truth on people's lives, not the truth about themselves or their past, but the Truth of all that Jesus has done for them.

At another conference a lady who had just had two years of counselling therapy commented that the Truth had done for her in two days what counselling had been unable to do in two years – set her free! You only had to look at her to see the evidence of what she was saying. Gone was the frown, the worried expression, the drawn and pinched look; she now appeared radiant and peaceful.

Surely it should not be difficult for Christians to find such joy when Jesus has already done everything necessary to set them free, no matter how damaged they have been or how horrendous their past experiences!

In this book I am going to share with you the essence of the teaching given at these conferences. I pray that as you read this book you will be directed afresh to the TRUTH that will set you free; and that you will see how God can use you to speak that Truth into others' lives that they too might enjoy 'the glorious liberty' of God's children.

2 The Wonderful Counsellor

God sent His Son, the Word of God, into the world to bring us the Truth. He came as the Light to speak into the spiritual darkness of the world.

Jesus came to us as God's Word, God's Truth, God's Wisdom. He came as the Wonderful Counsellor, the Holy Son of God.

Yet whenever Jesus spoke, a clear division took place between those who believed what He said and those who rejected His words, those who obeyed Him and those who denied Him. Often it was the religious people who refused to believe; they were so entrenched in their traditions that they could not recognise the Truth when they heard it! They were so busy being religious, they failed to recognise Him as their Messiah and Saviour, and so were not able to receive the life He offered them.

Yet prostitutes believed in Him and turned to Him; they recognised Him as the Holy One. Even swindlers and con-men received salvation. Beggars came and sat at His feet, cried out to Him and were healed by Him. Outcasts, demoniacs, lepers were set free by Him.

You would think that if the Holy One was walking around, the unholy wouldn't dare go near Him. Yet His holiness wasn't expressed in religious piety that repelled the world. His holiness attracted sinners; they were drawn to Him not because He said the things they wanted to hear, but what they needed to hear: the Truth. **The prostitutes, outcasts, swindlers, beggars and sick flocked to Him because He was the only Counsellor who had ever given them hope.** To the religious ones they were the scum of the earth, today's equivalent of the drug-pushers, the child abusers, the alcoholics.

They stood for hours in the hot sun to listen to Him teach, for here was someone who could get them into heaven despite what they were! **The Wonderful Counsellor didn't judge or condemn them but gave them a future and a hope.** No matter how depraved their lifestyles, no matter how inadequate they felt, even if they had lost all sense of self-worth, **here was someone who said they mattered!** Because they believed Him many of them went ahead of the religious ones into the Kingdom of heaven. They received the life Jesus came to give.

Jesus did not preach sentimentality, neither was He looking for an emotional response to His Gospel. He said:

> Enter through the narrow gate. For wide is the gate and broad is the road that leads to destruction, and many enter through it (Matt. 7:13).

He wanted to set people free from everything which bound them and caused destruction; and He wanted to give them God's life in all its fullness.

Here was the man who spoke the truth; the Wonderful Counsellor. The crowds flocked to hear Him, to hear the Truth that would set them free. He said:

> If you hold to my teaching, you are really my disciples. **Then you will know the truth, and the truth will set you free** (John 8:31–2).

The Truth will set you free from your depravity, your bondage, your unbelief, your guilt, your fear, your sickness. Whatever your need, **the Truth will set you free!** This was the message Jesus came to bring! **God's Kingdom life, eternal life, the fullness of life for you – NOW!**

As you read the Bible the Wonderful Counsellor is speaking to you with all the authority of God Himself. **If you need counsel, you can turn to Him and listen to His words, the words of the Wonderful Counsellor.** And you can be sure that everything He says to you will be true, for **He is the Truth!** Jesus said:

I am the way and the truth and the life (John 14:6).

Even His opponents recognised that He taught and acted with genuine authority. The religious ones could not match such authority.

ANOTHER COUNSELLOR

At the Last Supper His disciples were grief-stricken because the One in whom they had placed their hope was going to leave them. But He promised:

I will ask the Father, and he will give you another Counsellor to be with you for ever – the Spirit of truth (John 14:16–17).

The promised Counsellor, the Holy Spirit, is the Spirit of truth. Jesus had come with the words of truth, now He promised to give His followers the *Spirit* of truth. Although He was returning to the Father He promised that this other Counsellor would never be taken from them.

Jesus made it clear that 'the world cannot accept him, because it neither sees him nor knows him. But you know him, for he lives with you and will be in you' (John 14:17).

The Wonderful Counsellor was *with* them, but the other Counsellor would be *in* them.

If you are born again the Wonderful Counsellor, Jesus, will be with you always; and the other Counsellor, the Holy Spirit, will be in you always. The Counsellor lives in you! The Word of Truth is with you and the Spirit of Truth is in you. What more could you need? The Word and the Spirit together have the answer to every situation or need that could arise in your life. **Both these divine Counsellors will always agree together.** They are never at odds with one another.

When the Counsellor comes, whom I will send to you from the Father, the Spirit of truth who goes out from the Father, he will testify about me (John 15:26).

The ministry of the Holy Spirit living in you is to testify to you about Jesus. Why? Because the answer to every need in your life is contained in what Jesus has done for you. It is not some new technique of ministry or prayer that will set you free; **you simply need the Spirit of Truth to testify to you about Jesus.**

It is for your good that I am going away. Unless I go away, the Counsellor will not come to you; but if I go, I will send him to you . . . But when he, the Spirit of truth, comes, he will guide you into all truth (John 16:7,13).

Into what truth will the Holy Spirit guide us? The Truth of Jesus!

He will not speak on his own; he will speak only what he hears, and he will tell you what is yet to come. He will bring glory to me by taking from what is mine and making it known to you (John 16:13–14).

The Holy Spirit will never act independently of Jesus or the Father. There is always unity and agreement in the Trinity!

THE COUNSELLOR AT WORK

A woman was caught in bed with her lover. There could be no doubt that she was guilty of adultery. According to the law she should be stoned to death. The religious ones brought her to Jesus thinking that this time they could catch Him out. He claimed He had not come to overthrow the law but to fulfil it. Yet He had been preaching mercy, forgiveness and love. How could He reconcile such teaching when this woman deserved death? Jesus told them:

If any one of you is without sin, let him be the first to throw a stone (John 8:7).

On hearing this the people began to drift away beginning with the eldest, until Jesus was left alone with the woman.

'Has no-one condemned you?'
'No-one sir', she said.
'Then neither do I condemn you,' Jesus declared. 'Go now and leave your life of sin' (vv. 10–11).

'Religious' people are very good at judging others. Yet Jesus, who had the right to judge, had come to save and heal, not judge. He was not being soft with the woman; He was being merciful, expressing God's desire to forgive, not condemn. But He also made clear she was to leave her life of sin.

Like that woman we stand 'naked' before Jesus because He can see our hearts. He could judge us; but in His grace and mercy He wants to forgive us and set us free.

To believe Jesus is to receive eternal life; to disbelieve Him leaves a person in the condemnation we all deserve (John 3:16–18). In Him God has provided not only the Way of Salvation, but also the Truth that will enable us to live in the freedom He desires for His children. **Through the Wonderful Counsellor God sets us free completely from what we have been, and**

through the Holy Spirit He enables us to be what He wants us to be.

These are the Counsellors you need and if you are filled with the Holy Spirit, these are the Counsellors God has given you. They will work together for your total well-being, if only you are prepared to co-operate with them.

This book will show you how to do just that!

3   The Healing Nature of the Gospel

The Gospel is the good news of what God has done for us in Jesus Christ. Everything He said and did revealed His Father's character. Jesus said: 'Anyone who has seen me has seen the Father' (John 14:9). Jesus loves because it is God's nature to love. He is merciful and gracious because He reveals God's mercy and grace.

God alone has the right to judge sin because He alone is righteous by nature. Instead of sending His Son to judge He sent Him to save, to offer men the way out of the condemnation they deserve.

Jesus demonstrated His love for the world; He showed that it is His will to liberate people from bondage and to heal them in spirit, soul and body.

It is a common fallacy to say: 'Jesus accepts me just as I am.' Everyone is totally unacceptable to God in his or her natural state. 'All have sinned and fall short of the glory of God.' All are therefore under condemnation and will remain so eternally, unless they place their faith personally in the saving work of Jesus Christ. The good news is that we can be made acceptable to God, that we can live in a relationship with Him of total acceptance and love.

This is only possible for those who believe personally what

Jesus has said and done for them. Such faith makes them one with Jesus and they are able to share in His standing before God. Because He lived a life of total obedience when on earth, Jesus remained in a relationship of total acceptance and perfect unity with His Father. Those who believe in Him share that acceptance. **His life becomes their life, His acceptance their acceptance, His inheritance their inheritance.**

REPENT AND BELIEVE

The key to such a relationship is made clear by Jesus at the very beginning of His ministry:

> 'The time has come,' he said. 'The kingdom of God is near. Repent and believe the good news!' (Mark 1:15).

These are the two important keys Jesus gives us to a life of complete freedom in Him: repentance and faith.

Repentance involves much more than being sorry about your sins. It involves a complete change of mind and attitude. The one who repents turns away from a life of sin and has a completely new perspective on his life. He accepts God's goals and plans for his future, and submits to His purposes.

To repent, then, is to turn away from what you have been. Faith enables you to embrace the Truth of all that Jesus has done for you, so that you can enjoy the life He came to give you, becoming the person He wants you to be.

Repentance and faith are essential at the beginning of the Christian's life, for without these no one can be born again, enter God's Kingdom and receive the gift of eternal life. However, both repentance and faith need to be a way of life for every believer. There is little point in someone turning to Christ if he then turns back to his own ways. He needs to remain at one with Jesus, believing the Truth of what He has said and done for him.

The Christian who lives by these principles will walk in continual freedom. He will refuse to turn back to a self-centred life or to his past. He will remain turned to Christ. He will live the new life Jesus came to give him. Like Paul, he will 'reach out for that which lies ahead'. He will 'take hold of that for which Christ Jesus took hold of me' (Phil. 3:12).

You can be such a believer!

WRONG CONCEPTS OF GOD

Wrong attitudes to difficult circumstances often reflect wrong concepts of who God is. Many believe that God wants to punish them rather than be gracious to them; that He wants them to be sick instead of knowing Him as their Healer; that they are objects of His wrath rather than His mercy. They think it is impossible for them to please Him. Clearly they do not understand the status they have before Him through what Jesus has done for them. Instead they see themselves as spiritual failures, they feel useless and more aware of their negative attitudes than of His positive love!

For example, some claim it is difficult to think of God as 'Father' because of their catastrophic relationships with their human fathers. It is obvious that even the best, most loving father can in no way be compared to God in His love and Fatherhood. But emotions can be so powerful that they swamp reason.

When we look at events through the pain and hurt of negative emotions we inevitably have a distorted view of the Truth. However, when we begin with the revelation of Truth given us through Jesus, and then allow the truths of His Word to impact different areas of our lives, we discover that God views us in far more positive ways than we view ourselves.

It is a tragic mistake to begin with 'my own ideas of God'. That is to create a god after your own understanding. Such a god could not save or heal you, meet your needs or give you a sense of total well-being. **It is mistaken to judge God through the mishmash of your ever-changing emotions and circum-**

stances. You need to begin with the biblical revelation of who He is and allow the Truth of what He has done for you to influence your thinking and emotions. Jesus wants you to be free to enjoy the life He died to give you now. And He wants you to be certain that nothing could ever separate *you* from His love; that you will reign eternally with Him in His glory!

THE TRUE GOD

To describe who God is would require a book in itself, volumes even. All we can hope to do now is to touch on some key aspects of His nature crucial to our faith. Other aspects of His character will become clear later.

> The Lord, the Lord, the compassionate and gracious God, slow to anger, abounding in love and faithfulness, maintaining love to thousands, and forgiving wickedness, rebellion and sin (Exod. 34:6–7).

Of the multitude of scripture verses we could choose, we will begin with these words spoken by the Lord to reveal Himself to Moses. They point us to five key aspects of His character that are often emphasised in the scriptures.

Compassionate

God is compassionate. This means that He is not merely sympathetic, but merciful. Jesus did not come to heap pity on us; we have more than enough of self-pity already! To be compassionate is to 'suffer along with', to share in another's predicament. By sending Jesus to share our humanity God showed His compassion.

The God of the Old Testament is the same as the God of the New. Jesus came from heaven to give us a clear revelation of the nature and character of God. He showed compassion because His Father is compassionate by nature. He had compassion on the sick and healed them. He had compassion on the multitude and fed the people. **His compassion led to action, to definite results.**

Ultimately His compassion would lead Him to the cross!

Gracious

Jesus's compassion was expressed in the way He graciously gave of Himself to people.

Grace is the 'free, unmerited favour of God'. In simple terms it is **God giving His everything to those who deserve nothing.**

We are saved by grace, brought into a living relationship with God, by His activity – not through anything we have done for ourselves, or through any merit of our own. We could never deserve anything from Him. **He gives because He has chosen to give to those who trust in Jesus.** Everything we receive from Him is a demonstration of His grace. 'From the fulness of his grace we have all received one blessing after another' (John 1:16).

Only through our complete identification with Jesus (which will be explained later) are we able to receive the life and liberty He wants to give us.

Slow to Anger

Because death is His just and holy judgment on sin, God could wipe men from the face of the earth if He so chose. In His mercy and grace He has chosen not to do so, but has provided a way of escape from the judgment we deserve.

Even when we were spiritually dead and under condemnation because of our sins, **He chose not to vent His wrath on us, not to judge us as we deserve, but to offer us the way of salvation. He is slow to anger!** Through Jesus He draws us to Himself that we might experience His mercy and grace and come to know His love.

Those who are one with Jesus need have no fear of eternal punishment.

Abounding in Love

To know God is to know eternal and perfect love. His love is spiritual, not emotional. It is not based on feelings or circumstances, but on who He is. **God is love and therefore He loves. He loves because it is His nature to love.**

Many who seek counsel complain that they do not 'feel' loved by God. This is not surprising for such a statement suggests a basic misunderstanding about God. He is Spirit, not an emotion. **Once you believe in His love you experience His love, especially in the ways He cares and provides for you.** Having accepted His love, you may on occasions 'feel' His love, although such feelings are incidental and not the basis of a loving relationship with God. **It would be impossible to live the Christian life if we only believed in God's love for us when we had emotional feelings of being loved by Him!**

God 'abounds' in love. He overflows with love. So it cannot be difficult to know or receive that love together with the benefits accompanying such a privilege. And we shall see how we are able to do this.

Jesus did not demonstrate God's love by putting His arm around people and saying: 'There, there, it's all right! God loves you!' In fact He said remarkably little about love; He simply demonstrated it in action. And that love led Him, not only to identify totally with you in your need, but to give His life for you on the cross to liberate you from that need.

Abounding in Faithfulness

Not only does God abound in love towards us; He abounds in faithfulness. He is not begrudgingly faithful because He has given promises He must keep. It is His nature to be faithful. To deny His Word would be to deny Himself.

The Father will never deny His Son. He accepts all who put their faith in Him, regardless of what they have been or have done in the past. He will not turn away any who come to Him. **He honours the faith of all those who claim the efficacy of His blood to forgive their sins and meet every need in their lives.**

The Lord is faithful to His Word, and promises. He watches over His Word to perform it. He is faithful to all those who put their trust in Him. God is not fickle and does not change with moods! **Jesus Christ is the same yesterday and today and for ever; He reflects God's unchanging nature, that He is always totally reliable and dependable.**

Righteous

Because He is righteous by nature, God is righteous in all that He does. He is the standard by which everything and everyone is judged. **We could not be righteous before Him if it were not for Jesus and what He has done for us. He puts us right with His Father so we can approach Him with confidence. Those who are made righteous through Jesus have nothing to fear from the righteous God.**

This is the amazing work Jesus has accomplished through the cross: He makes righteous before God those who have been unrighteous and were previously totally unacceptable to Him. This is possible only because Jesus has offered to the Father the sacrifice of a totally righteous life on behalf of sinners, even though He was subjected to every temptation we can experience, was continually rejected, persecuted, falsely accused and even hated by those who opposed Him. He demonstrated the life of love in the midst of continual difficulty and then in love offered His life to the Father on our behalf. It is almost impossible for us to comprehend such love. But this is God's nature.

The Lord is righteous in all his ways and loving towards all he has made (Ps. 145:17).

He is Holy

Righteousness is one aspect of holiness. It is impossible for us to describe God's holiness adequately. He is whole, perfect and complete in Himself. He is therefore above and beyond all He has made.

Yet Jesus accepted the limitations of a human life and lived in holiness, full of mercy, full of grace, full of love, of joy, power and authority. **It is that fullness of life He gives to those who put their trust in Him.**

In everything He showed Himself submissive to the will of His Father:

For I have come down from heaven not to do my will but to do the will of him who sent me (John 6:38).

I do nothing on my own but speak just what the Father has taught me (John 8:28).

And so Jesus shows that submission to the will of His Father is an indispensable part of living a life of holiness on earth.

His purpose is that we should be like Him.

He chose us in him before the creation of the world to be holy and blameless in his sight (Eph. 1:4).

This is clearly not possible through any self-effort or personal achievement on our part. We cannot solve our own problems, let alone make ourselves holy! This is what God Himself will work within the believer, but only with his or her co-operation. To this end, God has made provision to deal with everything in our lives that is not like Him or is opposed to His purposes. **It is His intention to free you, therefore, from everything that is a hindrance to becoming more like Jesus. He is intent on changing you from one degree of glory to another.**

For those God foreknew he also predestined to be conformed to the likeness of his Son . . . (Rom. 8:29).

Therefore we do not lose heart. Though outwardly we are wasting away, yet inwardly we are being renewed day by day (2 Cor. 4:16).

It is good news that He who has begun a good work in you will bring it to completion! It is good news that God has made provision for you to become like He is!

MAN'S NATURE WITHOUT GOD

People are only ready to take hold of the good news if they first believe the bad news. This, stated simply, is to say that apart from Christ all are unacceptable to God and are living under condemnation. In other words they face judgment because of their sin.

> For all have sinned and fall short of the glory of God (Rom. 3:23).

Jesus Himself said: 'Whoever does not believe stands condemned already because he has not believed in the name of God's one and only Son' (John 3:18). What a contrast to those who do believe:

> I tell you the truth, whoever hears my word and believes him who sent me has eternal life and will not be condemned; he has crossed over from death to life (John 5:24).

God does not want to condemn; He wants to save and in Jesus has provided the only way of salvation. To receive this salvation involves passing from death to life.

Paul asserts that God 'wants all men to be saved and to come to a knowledge of the truth' (1 Tim. 2:4). Jesus makes it clear that this can only happen through faith in Him.

> I am the way and the truth and the life. No-one comes to the Father except through me (John 14:6).

Those who refuse to repent and believe are in grave danger:

But because of your stubbornness and your unrepentant heart, you are storing up wrath against yourself (Rom. 2:5).

How essential then, to repent and believe. **There can be no substitute for these two commands Jesus gives us.** They enable us to appropriate the life He offers, and then enable us to live in the fullness of that life.

There can be no substitute for His truth. Jesus warns His opponents:

But unless you *repent*, you too will all perish (Luke 13:5).

His opponents were very religious but they did not believe in Him. They sought to please God through self-righteousness instead of finding their true righteousness in Jesus. Again we see the contrast with those who accept Jesus:

Yet to all who received him, to those who *believed* in his name, he gave the right to become children of God (John 1:12).

Whoever *believes* in him shall not perish but have eternal life (John 3:16).

Whoever *believes* in him is not condemned (John 3:18).

Repent and believe. Repent and believe. Repent and believe. These are the keys to receiving all that God has to give us, including the freedom we are to enjoy as His children.

We dare not substitute anything for these two truths.

Counselling techniques can never replace obedience to the Truth Jesus proclaims. He has made clear that it is only by continuing to believe His words that we can be His disciples, know the Truth and enjoy the freedom He died to make possible for us. Jesus said this to those who believed in Him:

If you hold to my teaching, you are really my disciples. Then you will know the truth, and the truth will set you free (John 8:31–2).

THE ONLY WAY OF FREEDOM IS THE WAY OF TRUTH!

Every Christian needs to know the Truth, therefore, if he is to enjoy the freedom this alone brings. Those who desire to help others come into freedom need to do so in the way the Truth of God's Word indicates; not by taking people more deeply into themselves or into their past lives, but into the Truth. They need to know and understand the Truth that will set them free from sin and failure.

The Lord is near to all who call on him, to all who call on him *in truth* (Ps. 145:18).

Nothing can, or needs, to be added to what Jesus has already accomplished for us. **Faith in what He has said and done leads to complete freedom – from sin, past hurts, personal failure and inadequacy, bondages and sickness in all its forms.**

4   The Blood

In him we have redemption through his blood, the forgiveness of sins, in accordance with the riches of God's grace that he lavished on us with all wisdom and understanding (Eph. 1:7).

God created in love, and desires to have a relationship of love with those He made. Love is always vulnerable. Beings that can love must also have the capacity to hate.

God wants His people to obey Him as the outworking of their love for Him. They are to acknowledge His Lordship and supreme authority in their lives by willingly submitting themselves to Him. They have freedom to disobey, be stubborn and even rebellious. **God had to give them His complete freedom, with absolutely no restraint placed upon the use of their wills, or it would not have been possible for them to love.**

We know to our cost that Adam, and in Adam all mankind, came to a point of choosing self rather than God. He yielded to the temptation of the devil, who himself had acted similarly in heaven. Created as one of the celestial beings, subservient to the Lord, he was thrown out of heaven, having rebelled against God's authority, desiring to make himself the object of worship and admiration from others. Jesus said:

I saw Satan fall like lightning from heaven (Luke 10:18).

This was God's judgment. There could be no rebellious beings in heaven. The devil's purpose ever since has been to tempt mankind to follow him in his rebellion. Instead of serving the Lord he wants us to rebel against Him; instead of submitting to God's authority, he wants us to rise up in rebellious independence.

All of us were infected by Adam's sin: his rebellion tainted all mankind. All are born with a sinful nature and therefore inevitably sin! Even an innocent-looking baby is born with a sinful disposition, and it is not very long before he reveals it!

We are all aware of the drive within us to please self, to be the central focus of interest in our own lives. That drive tears man away from God's purposes and leads him into the sins of selfishness and self-indulgence, placing self instead of God on the throne of his life. Inevitably this causes a rift between man and God, an alienation within their relationship.

God had to rectify this situation. Man needed a Saviour to deliver him from his rebellion and foolishness. Even before the creation of the world God knew He would need to provide us with such a Saviour. He knew man would abuse the freedom He had given him. In His love, God decided not to do away with sinful humanity, although that is what mankind deserved. The story of Noah and the flood clearly shows us that God could so easily have wiped out humanity and started again; but this was not His purpose. **He wanted to redeem, to purchase back for Himself those who had been lost to Him because of their sin – everyone.**

God could not ignore sin as if it didn't matter. Because God's just and holy judgment on sin is the death penalty, someone who was Himself sinless had to suffer that death penalty, someone who was subjected to all the temptations we experience and yet remained innocent. **An innocent life had to be given on behalf of the guilty.** So Jesus purchased men for

God with the shedding of His blood, offering His own sinless life on behalf of sinful mankind.

Jesus obeyed the Father. He did everything that Satan failed to do and that man couldn't do. He pleased the Father in every way and in every detail. There was no charge that could be justly brought against Him. He was without sin, pure in every way. On the cross He shed His innocent, perfect and guiltless blood on behalf of sinners.

There are three ways in which we need to understand the significance of the shedding of Jesus's blood:

1 THE BLOOD WAS SHED FOR GOD

This was the price God required in order that all our sin, and everything in our lives that had destroyed fellowship with Him, could be forgiven and cleansed. **The righteous requirements of God have been satisfied by the blood of His Son.**

Because all had sinned and fallen short of God's glory, no man could make such an offering. The only way such a sacrifice could be provided was by God becoming man Himself. **This is the evidence of His amazing love; that He saw the complete helplessness and hopelessness of man's situation, and so became man in Jesus.**

Jesus offered Himself to the Father on our behalf. It is only because He shed His blood that we can know God as our Father and receive His forgiveness for our sins.

No man can inflict crucifixion on himself. Jesus was not allowed to take a route of self-destruction. The manner of His death had to be inflicted on Him by those for whom He died. So He was unjustly accused, unjustly condemned, and unjustly nailed to a cross; and yet He prayed:

Father, forgive them, for they do not know what they are doing (Luke 23:34).

When we consider the meaning of the cross we shall see that it is very significant that suicide was not permitted. Many Christians today try to put their old natures to death, instead of realising that they have been crucified with Christ.

In the blood, our heavenly Father sees the holy, perfect and innocent offering of total self-giving love. When He looks upon any individual man, woman or child, He sees a sinner; He sees the rebellion, all that is unholy, ungodly, and unrighteous. He knows about the independence, pride, lust, jealousy and greed. He sees it all.

But when someone believes in the blood of Jesus, He sees not the sinner but the innocence, the perfection, and the worthiness of the blood. No one comes into relationship with God the Father without that blood.

There is never a day in your life, never an hour, a minute, a second, a moment of time when you have any other means of access to God except by the blood. Many believers lose sight of this basic truth: **I could not even dare to speak to God today if it was not for the blood of Jesus.** The ground of my acceptance is always His blood.

If I ever try to come into God's presence on any basis other than the blood, I have fallen into error because I am coming not in His virtue but in some virtue of my own. I am coming on my own terms, on my own ground, on my own initiative rather than by the means of my acceptance by Him.

2 THE BLOOD IS SHED FOR US

When we approach God through the blood, He sees us through the virtue of the blood; innocent, made worthy, righteous, and holy. Christians talk in negative unbelief about themselves only because they do not understand what Jesus has done for them in the shedding of His blood. They concentrate on their unworthiness rather than on His grace and mercy through which they have been made worthy. They feel unacceptable and unable to enter the Holy of Holies **'with a sincere heart in full assurance of faith'** (Heb. 10:22).

There is absolutely nothing you can do, or need to do, to deserve God's acceptance, love or blessings. Jesus has already done everything for you! The fundamental problem for many Christians is that they do not truly believe God has totally forgiven and accepted them through Jesus's blood. There is no point in looking at themselves and their unacceptability. They can only fix their eyes on Jesus and marvel at this miracle of grace.

To live in the power of Jesus's blood is to live every day in His freedom. Paul said:

It is for freedom that Christ has set us free (Gal. 5:1).

You are set free from sin, guilt, fear, from bondage to Satan and even self when you put your faith in what He has done for you in the shedding of His blood! He wants to see you walking in that freedom, not in condemnation.

Because of your faith in Jesus's blood, the Father says: 'I forgive you.' This is the expression of His grace, mercy and love for you.

He also wants to reproduce in you that same forgiving grace, so that when others sin you forgive them. He is merciful to you, so you are to be merciful to others.

The shedding of Jesus's blood satisfies every need. Nothing is beyond the power of the blood; no sin, sickness, or need. Every negative is dealt with.

3 THE BLOOD ANSWERS EVERY ACCUSATION OF SATAN

The devil is described as *the accuser of the brethren*. Sin gives him ground for accusation. Why is there no condemnation for those who are in Christ Jesus? Because once forgiven, Satan's ground of accusation is removed from under his feet. **He has no valid accusation against those made righteous through Jesus's blood.** Even when a believer sins he is forgiven and cleansed from all unrighteousness once he has confessed his sin. He is restored to the place of innocence, righteousness and worthiness in God's sight, and Satan cannot rightly accuse him!

The devil will never be forgiven. As a believer you always stand on higher ground! **You do not have to listen to any of his lies or accusations. Instead, you can be thankful for your complete forgiveness. The Lord keeps no record of your wrongs.** There will be no mention of them on the Day of Judgment. You are forgiven!

You are so totally acceptable to God that He has come to live in you, and you live in Him. He sees you as now made holy with direct access into the Holy of Holies.

Because of the blood you need not fear God's wrath or punishment. **Jesus suffered the punishment you deserve and now you can live at peace with Him.**

Praise God for the precious, holy, life-giving blood of Jesus!

5 The Cross

> I have been crucified with Christ and I no longer live, but Christ lives in me. The life I live in the body, I live by faith in the Son of God, who loved me and gave himself for me. I do not set aside the grace of God, for if righteousness could be gained through the law, Christ died for nothing! (Gal. 2:20–1).

God has not only made it possible for our sins to be forgiven; He has dealt with the root cause of our sin.

We are all aware of internal conflicts. It seems sometimes as if a great spiritual battle is being fought within us. The Holy Spirit is urging us to believe and obey God's Word. At the same time something within us is trying to drag us back into sin, tempting us to please self and walk in the flesh.

This conflict did not exist before your new birth. When it was your nature to sin, you did so without any reference to God's purpose for your life. The Righteous One was not living within you causing you to feel uncomfortable about your sin. Now, however, the Holy Spirit living within you warns you not to sin and convicts you when you do! He urges you to be restored to a right relationship with God.

When you first believed the Gospel, God put you into Christ and placed the Spirit of Christ in you.

And you also were included in Christ when you heard the word of truth, the gospel of your salvation. Having believed, you were marked in him with a seal, the promised Holy Spirit, who is a deposit guaranteeing our inheritance (Eph. 1:13–14).

Notice the sequence here:

1 **You heard the word of Truth, the Gospel of salvation.** You may have heard through reading the Bible, listening to a sermon or a friend testifying. One way or another you *heard.*

2 **You believed what you heard.** Faith was essential for the message to become effective in your life.

3 **He incorporated you into Christ as a work of His grace,** but not until you believed!

4 **God demonstrated that you had His 'seal of approval' by giving you the Holy Spirit.** So God now lives in you.

5 **Your eternal inheritance is guaranteed.** You do not need to fear the future or even death. Your eternal destiny is assured.

You are in the Righteous One and the Righteous One is in you. No wonder you feel uneasy, when you realise you have grieved Him. No wonder you experience conflict! This is the inevitable result of the Holy Spirit's presence within you. But if you condemn yourself because of this conflict, you are placing yourself under false condemnation.

DEAD

God has done everything to enable you to have victory in this conflict. When Jesus went to the cross He took not only the sins we committed; He took us, the sinners. 'I have been crucified with Christ!' says Paul.

The weak, jealous, self-centred, sinful 'I' was crucified with

Christ! **That person no longer exists.** This was true for Paul, it is true for you also. God did not incorporate into Christ the sinner you were, but the new creation you are now!

A Christian lives by faith in what God has already done for him. Jesus has not only died for you; **you have died with Him.**

> Don't you know that all of us who were baptised into Christ Jesus were baptised into his death? We were therefore buried with him through baptism . . . (Rom. 6:3).

Water baptism signifies that the person you once were is not only put to death but has been buried with Christ. The old life is dead, buried and finished with. You are now a new creation. A new person came into being when you were born again. You cannot be born again unless the person that you were has first died!

Faith is being sure of what we hope for and certain of what we do not see (Heb. 11:1). **God wants you to be sure and certain that you have died and that your life is now hidden with Christ in God!** He does not tell you that you have to put yourself to death; Jesus has put your old nature to death with Him on the cross!

Instead of believing the old life has gone, many turn to counselling and prayer techniques which take them back into the past which is dead! Understanding your past will not enable you to live a victorious new life. We dare not substitute any method of ministry for faith in what God has done.

You are to reckon yourself dead to the old life and alive in Christ. Going back into the old can never enable you to live the new life. The secret of living in victory is to know that you have been separated from your past, that you have died with Christ and are now living a new life in Him. There can be no substitute for faith. As Paul says: 'The life I now live in the body I live by *faith* in the Son of God who loved me and gave Himself for me'!

Your feelings, thoughts and experiences will sometimes

seem to deny the Truth, and later we shall see how to believe the Truth in the face of all those things which oppose faith.

A NEW LIFE

Jesus took you to the cross to make it possible for you to receive a new life. It is no longer your nature to sin; you have a new nature: **'Christ in you!'** He has given you His Spirit to enable you to live this new life.

You can walk in righteousness as you continue to trust in Jesus and what He has done for you. If you do not live the new life you will inevitably sink back into the old. It is potentially possible for every decision, every action, and every word to be done 'in Christ', as you learn to follow the leading of the Holy Spirit.

Yet the way many Christians see themselves, and the way they feel about themselves, seems to deny this totally. They fail so often that they wonder at times whether they could really have been placed in Christ. They remain self-centred, victims of their negative feelings because they do not believe the old has gone!

Jesus said you would be tempted, but God will ensure that you will never be tempted beyond your ability to endure or resist. **You have died, but sin hasn't!**

God has put into you the resources to say 'No' to sin; you can resist temptation and anything that grieves the Lord. It is never true for a Christian to say, 'I couldn't help it'. The sinner sins because it is his nature to sin. A believer can choose to sin but it is no longer his nature to sin. He has the choice to please God or himself. If he continues to make the wrong choices he can find sin irresistible; but that's only the result of a pattern he has allowed to develop. He has given himself to a particular sin so much that it has become a habit and is working death in him; whereas the Spirit wants to work life in him. **He is a new creation but lives as if in the grip of old patterns of behaviour.**

In the old life you were susceptible to any temptation. The

devil could manipulate and use you because there was no righteousness within you. You yielded easily to the temptations and desires of the flesh in order to please self. Now you have the choice of living in the old life or the new, of walking in the Spirit, pleasing God, or in the flesh, pleasing self.

Although crucified with Christ, this does not mean you will automatically walk in the Spirit. The only way to resolve this conflict between the flesh and the Spirit is by faith! It cannot be done through prayer alone; it can only be accomplished by faith, which begins by believing what God has done for us in Christ.

If we have been united with him like this in his death, we will certainly also be united with him in his resurrection. **For we know** that our old self was crucified with him (Rom. 6:5–6).

We know this. We are sure and certain of it. **The old life was put to death with Him.** We no longer have to yield to the temptation of sin. We no longer have to walk in independence or selfishness. We know this! Those living in the past or who keep raking up the past, do not believe this Truth. **They cannot walk in the assurance of the new life if they don't believe that Jesus has already dealt the death blow to their old life.**

FREE FROM SIN

We know that we were crucified with Him so that the body of sin, which wants to do all the things that oppose God, is done away with.

. . . Anyone who has died has been freed from sin (Rom. 6:7).

If you feel that you are losing the battle against the conflict within you, it is because you do not believe you have been freed from sin. Not only are your sins forgiven; you have been freed from sin!

The death he died, he died to sin once for all; but the life he lives, he lives to God. **In the same way, count yourselves dead to sin but alive to God in Christ Jesus** (Rom. 6:10–11).

Jesus only had to die once to accomplish salvation for all mankind. The crucifixion was an event in history that will never have to be repeated. **In the same way** you have died to sin once and for all! That too is an historical event; it happened when Jesus died. You died with Him. So you are not to keep trying to put yourself to death. HE HAS ALREADY DONE THAT. **You no longer live!** What a relief!

Sin ruled in that old life. Jesus is to rule in the new life. Sin hasn't died; but you have died to sin. That is as much an accomplished fact as the crucifixion.

Other people can still hurt and fail me, but I don't have to react with bitterness and anger because it is no longer 'I' who live but Christ who lives in me. He lives in me in love. He will enable me to forgive, to bless even those who hate me, to express His life through my life. The old life that was a contradiction to His life is now dead and buried. I can choose to sin, but I am no longer bound by my old sinful nature. **My new nature is Christ in me, the hope of glory!**

It is at once obvious that neither you nor I manifest the new life perfectly. Understanding my old life will not enable me to live the new. Going back into what is dead cannot possibly enable me to live the new life. As Paul says, the life I now live must be lived by faith in Jesus Christ! You are not to dig up or resurrect what is dead and buried with Christ.

The devil wants you to do just that. He wants you to believe that you are not truly crucified with Christ, that the old has not passed away, that you are still in bondage to sin. If you believe him you will keep looking back, thinking that somehow the answer to the freedom you desire lies in trying to unravel your past. This is the devil's snare. He will point to the fact that you sin so readily and have so many hurt feelings and bad memories that you could not possibly have died with Christ.

To believe the devil is to deny the Truth. And Jesus says that it is the Truth that will set you free. The enemy knows how to keep a person in bondage: tempt him to believe his feelings, his fears, his experiences, and so deny the Truth of what God has done for him.

You are called to 'live by faith in the Son of God' – not the devil's lies! So do not set aside what God has graciously done for you. **In His love Jesus took the old, hurt, disobedient, rebellious, rejected failure that you were and put you to death on the cross.** Now He has come to live in you to enable you to live the new life.

Hear it again: **'You died, and your life is now hidden with Christ in God'** (see Col. 3:3). Ask the Holy Spirit to give you revelation of this wonderful Truth. You have died. Don't do anything that would deny this great Truth. Your water baptism was the funeral service of your old life. It has gone, and good riddance!

6 In Christ

Occasionally I have heard people say that they long to have such an intimate relationship with God that they will be able to add to the revelation of scripture. Such is the pride of man! Who could possibly add to what God has already accomplished in Jesus? Those who say such things demonstrate that they do not understand what He has already done. It is complete. We only await His return for the total fulfilment of all He has promised, and only God Himself knows when that event will take place!

We do not have to seek for any revelation beyond that which God has given us in His Word. Any true prophetic word will guide us into a further understanding and application of the Truth of His Word in our lives, for the Holy Spirit is the Spirit of Truth who guides us into all the Truth of His Word. He takes the things of Jesus and declares them to us.

ST DEFEATED

We are products of our experience, circumstances and the influence of people around us. Many see themselves as victims of their past. They feel condemned to a life of failure and rejection, as their track record shows. Certain patterns of negativity have become so deeply ingrained in them that they can see no way of ever being different, even though they may profess faith in Jesus Christ.

This certainly should not be the case, and does not need to be so. Suppose someone who claims to be born again and to have received the Holy Spirit comes to you and says: 'I'm no good. I'm just a failure. I always get things wrong. I constantly fail God. I know He wouldn't want to heal me. He certainly couldn't use me to perform a miracle in anyone else's life.' At such a tirade of negativity you would know immediately that this is not humility but the product of unbelief. Your objective would not be to condemn or judge the person who is weak in faith, **but to encourage him to see the Truth about his life now that he is in Christ.**

It may be his initial response to the Truth is negative: 'Oh, I can't believe. I have been rejected so often that I fear God will reject me. I dare not ask Him for anything in case He refuses me. He must think I am awful. How can He possibly love me? And if He does, why has He allowed so much trouble in my life?'

This all-too-common scenario points again to alarming unbelief and even self-deception. Again it is not our business to judge but to help. We will not do that by trying to help the person to understand his past experiences of rejection, failure and futility. We need to lead him into the Truth that will change his own perception of himself, so that he no longer sees himself as a hopeless failure, but as one who can lead a liberated and triumphant life.

Such a thought may seem totally beyond him, but this is because he does not recognise the Truth about himself now that he is born again. Perhaps he is ignorant of the Truth, so cannot understand. It is not prayer that he needs initially but a good dose of the Truth. This diagram will help us to understand the nature of the problem and how it can be overcome. I want to emphasise that we are talking here about someone who is born again, who has yielded his or her life to Jesus

Christ and has received the gift of the Holy Spirit. He is therefore a 'saint', but feels that he is St Desperate or St Defeated. He is certainly not St Victorious!

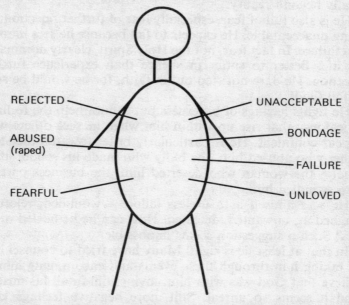

How does he view himself? He tries to believe he is accepted, but *feels* rejected. He has a long case history of rejection which, let us say, began in early childhood when deserted by his father or mother. The ensuing divorce and rejection by a step-parent caused deep unhappiness. There was rejection at school from one particular teacher whom he could never please; rejection also from other children who bullied him. He was jilted when he had finally managed to commit himself to a relationship; and then, to crown everything, he felt totally rejected by his minister and church who seemed so wrapped up in their activities that they had no time for him. So saint he may be (according to God's Word), but he must be St Rejected!

No matter how many times well-meaning Christians now put their arms around him and tell him that he is loved, his feelings tell him that such a suggestion, though desirable, is totally beyond reality.

He is also full of fear, especially fear of further rejection, of being unacceptable. He expects to fail because he sees himself as a failure. In fact fear, not the Holy Spirit, clearly dominates his life. Better to suffer in silence than experience further rejection. He dare not step out in faith, for he would be sure to fail God!

He fights feelings of bitterness but cannot help the feelings of jealousy that rise up within him when he sees others who appear confident. He is particularly bitter towards the stepfather who abused him, the bully who made his school life a misery, the woman who deserted him, the business partner who swindled him.

He sees himself as a useless failure – wounded, rejected, laughed at, unwanted, defeated. How can he be healed of all this? Such a suggestion seems impossible.

In that at least he is right! Many have tried to counsel him by taking him through these events and encouraging him to believe that God was with him, loving him in all his misery. And it seems so unreal. Still more negative feelings keep coming to the surface, more negative memories that need to be dealt with. He is taken farther and farther back in experience, but all to no avail. If he is honest he still *feels* the same. He has appreciated the time and attention given him, but he does not see himself as being any different. He is comforted to a measure by the fact that God knows all about his seemingly endless ordeal, but perplexed as to why He doesn't do anything about it. What a picture of negativity he is!

Of course, God does not need to do anything to liberate St Defeated or St Rejected or St Hopeless; He has already done it! God clearly states this. Let us point St Defeated towards the Truth.

When he was born again he became a new creation. His old life passed away and he was given a new life (2 Cor. 5:17). He died and his life is now hidden with Christ in God. His water baptism signified that he was dead and lay buried with Christ (Rom. 6:4). The person he was before his new birth no longer exists, therefore. So it seems nonsensical to take him back over a past that no longer exists, to encourage him to understand a person who is now dead and lies buried!

The scripture affirms that he is a son of God, that the Lord forgave him all his sins when he turned to Him in repentance. He is now righteous in God's sight; but all this seems totally unreal in the light of his feelings about himself. He reads that God has blessed him in Christ with every spiritual blessing in heaven (Eph. 1:3), that he has come to fullness of life because he is in Christ (Col. 2:10), that he has everything he needs for life and godliness, that God *always* leads him in triumph through Christ – and it all seems so unreal in the light of his feelings and his own concept of himself.

Of course, unwittingly, **he has been encouraged in this low self-image by all those who have helped him probe the secrets of his past failures and hurts. They have simply joined him in denying the person he now is in Christ.** They have aided him in denying the Truth instead of believing it.

So the truth, or his limited understanding of it, remains as head knowledge. He needs it in his heart, which still seems so full of negativity. He agrees wholeheartedly with those who assert that this journey from the head to the heart is the longest journey in the world!

How can these things be true, for one who is so full of negativity?

Without realising it he is living a lie, and those who have directed him back into the past have helped him in that lie. He does not understand the truth of who he is as a born-again believer.

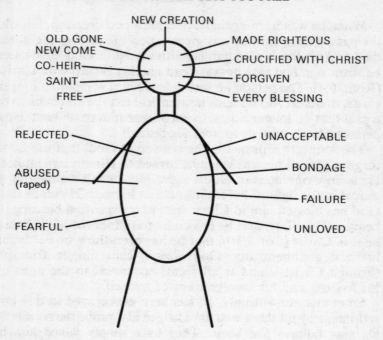

THE TRUTH

'For he has rescued us from the dominion of darkness and brought us into the kingdom of the Son he loves' (Col. 1:13) The Kingdom of God is now within him.

Jesus is in him, for 'the secret is this: Christ in you, the hope of glory' (Col. 1:27).

God Himself has come to take up residence within him in the person of the Holy Spirit. His body is, then, a temple of the Holy Spirit.

The truth is that he is not filled with rejection, failure, fear etc., but with God, the life of His Spirit and His Kingdom. All those things he has received only as head knowledge are certainly true and they are his route to true freedom. He is not to look back, but to the Truth. He is not to look at himself but at the Truth! He is to fix his eyes on Jesus, not take an occasional glance at Him (Heb. 12:2). He is to set his heart and mind on things above, not on earthly things – including himself.

Above all, he is to reckon himself dead and made alive in Christ.

First, however, he must realise that his feelings and many of his thoughts (prompted by the enemy) are lying to him. **He is not who he feels he is, but who God says he is. When he believes what God says, his feelings about himself will change because his perception about himself will be different.** The Truth will set him free from his negativity. While he persists in thinking of himself as a failure he will continue to live as a failure.

FACTS AND TRUTH

St Defeated is confused because he wrongly believes facts to be the truth. Let me explain by giving a simple example.

A born-again believer is told by his doctor that he has cancer and has only a short time to live. He is shown X-rays which show clearly the existence of the tumour. He feels the symptoms in his body. Clearly the facts indicate he has cancer. It would be foolish of him to deny these facts and claim the cancer didn't exist.

These are the facts, but not the Truth! The Truth is that by the stripes of Jesus he is healed. The facts state he has cancer; the Truth says he is healed. Which is he to believe?

The facts are natural; the Truth is supernatural. The supernatural is far more powerful than the natural! He has to choose, then, whether he is to put his faith in the facts or the Truth, in the natural or the supernatural.

The Truth is able to change the facts but the facts can never change the Truth. So a believer can trust in the natural prognosis or in the Truth.

Truth is a person: Jesus! He said: 'I am the Truth', and, 'the Truth will set you free'.

St Defeated's history is a series of facts of events he has

experienced. It would be foolish to suggest these things had never happened! But they are not the Truth about him now that he lives in Christ and Christ in him. He needs to concentrate on the spiritual, supernatural Truth that has changed the facts and made him a new creation. The more he concentrates on the facts, the more he will deny the Truth of what God has done for him in Christ.

He needs the help of those who will build him up in the Truth, not help him to deny it by concentrating on facts of the past which are not the Truth about him now. **How can he be expected to believe in who he is now, if people are helping him to deny his new identity by encouraging him to believe the rejected, hurt, weak and useless failure is still alive. He is not! That person is dead and buried, crucified with Christ. Realising this is at the heart of his victory.**

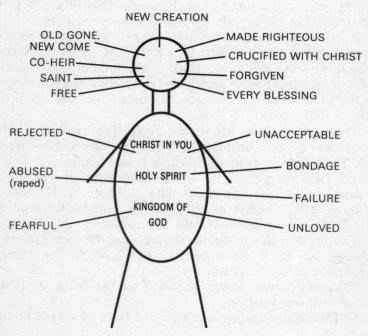

At the time of the crucifixion Paul was an enemy of Christ; later he came to understand that he had been crucified with Christ. Jesus did not have to die again when Paul became a believer. He accepted then what Jesus had done years before, when Paul was still an unbeliever.

When Jesus went to the cross He took every sinner with Him; 'one died for all, and therefore all died' (2 Cor. 5:14).

This is supernatural truth that can change the natural! When Jesus went to the cross He took you with Him.

Jesus Christ identified totally with you so that you could be identified totally with Him! His death became your death, so that His life might become your life.

HEALING?

Your old life does not need to be healed; it is dead! The dead cannot be healed! Neither do they need to be! The good news is that you are not the person that was born into the world, but the new person that was born when you put your faith in Jesus. At that point you appropriated what He did for you on the cross.

You do not have to try to kill the old life; it is already crucified with Christ.

For you died, and your life is now hidden with Christ in God (Col. 3:3).

Therefore, if anyone is in Christ, he is a new creation; the old has gone, the new has come! (2 Cor. 5:17)

The old life of sin has gone. When you came to Christ, giving your life to Him, you came in repentance recognising that you had sinned and needed God's forgiveness. **When you confessed your sins, He forgave you completely and eradicated the past with all its failure.**

In him we have redemption through his blood, the forgiveness of sins, in accordance with the riches of God's grace (Eph. 1:7).

Not only did He forgive you, but He made you righteous in His sight. You were 'justified', made totally acceptable in God's sight, not because of what you had done but because of what He had done for you. **The old was totally unacceptable; the new totally accepted!**

> God made him who had no sin to be sin for us, so that in him we might become the righteousness of God (2 Cor. 5:21).

> How much more, then, will the blood of Christ . . . cleanse our consciences from acts that lead to death, so that we may serve the living God! (Heb. 9:14).

You have been made righteous in God's sight; you can serve Him in love and freedom! You only have to believe the Truth!

7 Spirit, Soul, Body

It is important to understand how spirit, soul and body operate in relation to one another. Your soul, often described as your personality, has three principal functions:

1 **Your mind or intellect,** giving you the ability to reason and understand.
2 **Your emotions or feelings** which are affected considerably by your thinking.
3 **Your will;** your ability to make choices or decisions. In the soul life this ability is influenced greatly by both your thinking and feelings.

Before your new birth you were spiritually dead. It was as if your human spirit was in a coma waiting to be brought to life by God's Spirit. This happened when you were born again.

God is Spirit and therefore He makes direct contact with us through our human spirits. It was not possible for you to have a spiritual relationship with Him until your new birth. At that moment His Spirit came to live in your spirit.

Jesus made it clear that a person must be born of the Spirit if he is to see God's Kingdom. He knew that it was possible to serve God, love Him even, with the soul; but this did not make a person spiritually alive.

Among many Christians there is considerable confusion between the soul and the spirit; some even erroneously equate the two. Paul says:

> May your whole spirit, soul and body be kept blameless at the coming of our Lord Jesus Christ. The one who calls you is faithful and he will do it (1 Thess. 5:23–4).

Clearly he sees a distinction between the soul and spirit and asserts firmly that God Himself will ensure both are kept blameless! In Hebrews we read:

> For the word of God is living and active. Sharper than any double-edged sword, it penetrates even to dividing soul and spirit, joints and marrow; it judges the thoughts and attitudes of the heart (Heb. 4:12).

In dividing for us the soul and spirit, the Word shows us what is of self (the soul) and what is truly of God, working through the Spirit.

The following diagrams help us to understand the relationship between spirit, soul and body. Before you were born again, your soul and body acted independently of God. You may have wanted to live a 'good' life; or you may have lived a very immoral and ungodly life. In either case your soul and body acted independently of God. You may not even have believed in His existence. If you did, you still made decisions without a heart submission to the Lord and therefore to His purposes.

Your body houses both your spirit and soul but cannot take any actions without direction from your soul. So, before your new birth the following represents the way you functioned:

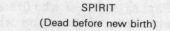

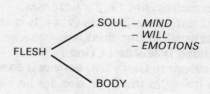

THE FLESH

When the soul and body act independently of God this is called in the New Testament, 'living in the flesh'. It must be remembered that **your flesh can do many seemingly good things, but independently of God.**

In the world you are surrounded by people who live 'in the flesh', with no submission to God and His purposes. Obviously many of them do 'good' things. They can be loving and care for others. They can be very religious, but without submission to the Lordship of Jesus Christ in their lives. Before your new birth you lived 'in the flesh' because it was then your nature to do so.

Now we must see what the scriptures say about this 'flesh' life, the soul and body acting independently of God.

1   Jesus said: **'The Spirit gives life; the flesh counts for nothing'** (John 6:63). Most people do not believe that this self-life, with all its 'good' and religious activity, counts for nothing in God's sight. Nevertheless this is the truth, for nothing that *we* do can make us acceptable to God. We cannot be saved either by our good deeds, or by our religious activities and observances. This was a bitter pill for the very religious Pharisees to swallow!

2   In Romans 8, Paul says: **'Those who live according to the
    sinful nature have their minds set on what that nature
    desires'** (v. 5). Those who want to please themselves
    maintain their independence. Their thinking revolves
    around themselves, not God's purposes.

3   **The mind of sinful man is death** (v. 6). It is spiritual death
    to be self-centred in our thinking.

4   **The sinful mind is hostile to God** (v. 7).

5   **It does not submit to God's law, nor can it do so** (v. 7). Even
    if a person living 'in the flesh' decides he wants to please
    God, he finds he is unable to do so.

6   **Those controlled by the sinful nature cannot please God**
    (v. 8). They may want to do away with the obviously bad
    or wicked things that self can perpetrate; but they still
    want self to dominate their lives. They want to be
    independent, to be in control!

7   Paul recognised that: **'I know that nothing good lives in me,
    that is, in my sinful nature'** (7:18). His estimate of the value
    of the flesh agrees with what Jesus said: 'Apart from me
    you can do nothing' (John 15:5).

8   Therefore Paul urges us to **'put no confidence in the flesh'**
    (Phil. 3:3). Put no confidence in this self-life, in soulish-
    ness. It is completely unreliable.

9   **Those who please God do not walk according to the flesh,
    but according to the Spirit.** Because you have been
    crucified with Christ, you no longer have to walk in
    the flesh. Because you have received the Holy Spirit,
    you can walk in the Spirit.

10 We now have to face an uncomfortable truth. Before
    you were born again it was natural or instinctive for you
    to walk in the flesh, for life to be centred around self.
    **Now that you are born again and Jesus lives in you, your
    life is to be centred on Him.** However, you can still choose
    to please self instead. Before you were in spiritual
    bondage and instinctively pleased self. Now you are
    freed from that bondage but can still choose to please

self instead of God. He will never take away your ability to choose. If He did so it would be impossible for you to love.

If you do not accept God's estimate of the flesh, you will continue to walk in it. Jesus did not try to reform your flesh life; He took it to the cross and put it to death, so that you can be liberated from it. As far as God is concerned the flesh is so corrupt and deceived that it cannot be reformed, only put to death.

THE ANSWER TO THE FLESH

Every believer has to accept this death of his self-life. So Paul asserts:

11 **Those who belong to Christ 'have crucified the sinful nature with its passions and desires'** (Gal. 5:24). Anyone who is born again belongs to Christ. The believer does not have to crucify himself. **He is already crucified!** Yes, even the passions and desires of the flesh have gone to the cross.

The believer has crucified the flesh, not by trying to put himself to death, but by recognising that when Christ died, he died also. Everything that belonged to that self-life, and is therefore in opposition to God's purposes, has been put to death by virtue of what Jesus Christ has done.

To fight your self-life only stirs it up – the very opposite of recognising that you have died with Christ. To delve into your life before you were born again is to suggest that you were not truly crucified with Christ, that His work for you was somehow incomplete, that there is something you have to do to add to what He has done for you.

12 It is not only a question of reckoning that self-life crucified with Christ, but also of putting on the life He gives you:

> **Clothe yourself with the Lord Jesus Christ, and do not think about how to gratify the desires of the sinful nature.** (Rom. 13:14).

Paul deals with this more fully in Colossians:

> **Put to death, therefore, whatever belongs to your earthly nature** (3:5).

He then lists several works of the flesh which are objects of God's wrath:

> You used to walk in these ways, in the life you once lived. But now you must rid yourself of all such things as these: anger, rage, malice, slander and filthy language from your lips. Do not lie to each other, **since you have taken off your old self with its practices** and have put on the new self, which is being renewed in knowledge in the image of its Creator (vv. 7–10).

To say that your old life has been crucified with Christ is to acknowledge that 'you have taken off the old self with its practices'.

This need not be confusing if you realise that the Truth is like two sides of the coin:

The Objective Truth is that when Jesus went to the cross He took you with Him. Your old self-life was crucified with Him.

The Subjective Truth is that you have to believe this is what He did and then realise that **you can 'put to death therefore' whatever belongs to that self-life: not fight it, stir it up, look at it, talk about it, but deny it by reckoning it as dead.** It is essential to concentrate, not on fighting the old, but on putting on the new!

> In the same way, **count yourselves dead to sin but alive to God in Christ Jesus.** Therefore do not let sin reign in your mortal body so that you obey its evil desires. Do not offer the parts

of your body to sin, as instruments of wickedness, but rather offer yourselves to God, **as those who have been brought from death to life;** and offer the parts of your body to him as instruments of righteousness (Rom. 6:11–13).

It is clear that the only way for a Christian to live is by faith: 'The righteous will live by faith' (Rom. 1:17). In the Gospel a righteousness from God is revealed, 'a righteousness that is by faith from first to last'. **Faith believes that you were crucified with Christ.**

The life I live in the body, I live by faith in the Son of God, who loved me and gave himself for me (Gal. 2:20).

I am no longer bound by my past. I no longer have to allow 'self' to dominate my life. Now I am free to follow Christ and to live a life pleasing to Him. I will do this, not by fighting what is dead, but by concentrating on the new life He has given me. **I do not have to try and improve that 'self' life; I am free to live the new.**

THE NEW LIFE

Let us extend the diagram to see how we can live this new life given to us in Christ.

The Holy Spirit now lives in your spirit; you are alive spiritually. Your body is the vehicle for doing God's will, but cannot act without direction from your soul. As you submit your soul to be governed by His Spirit, He will inform your mind of His will. **God has given you a mind not to argue with Him, but to be able to understand what He says to you and translate it into action.**

Your soul needs to be submitted to the Spirit, therefore. Then even your emotions will be brought under the authority of the Spirit. You will no longer be governed by feelings (which are unpredictable and unreliable) but by the Holy Spirit.

HOLY SPIRIT

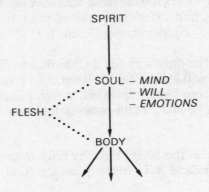

The key word here is 'submission'. While the soul and body remain submitted to your spirit (working in conjunction with the Holy Spirit) you are in God's order. But if you choose to please 'self' (to walk in the flesh) you elevate the soul above the spirit; you are then out of order:

GOD'S ORDER: SPIRIT   OUT OF ORDER: SOUL
                SOUL   SPIRIT
                BODY   BODY

When you are out of God's order your spirit is crushed, the Holy Spirit grieved, and self (the soul) is placed in the dominant position.

Remember, the soul is capable of doing many religious, good and seemingly worthy things, but if they are done independently of God they count for nothing. They serve only to elevate self.

It is clear that many Christians strive to please God by soulish activity. What they do is determined by what they want to do for God, instead of submitting themselves to Him and His direction for their lives.

JESUS'S TEACHING

Jesus Himself made it clear what is to be done with this soul life. (The Greek word can be translated either 'life' or 'soul'):

> **Whoever finds his life [soul] will lose it, and whoever loses his life [soul] for my sake will find it** (Matt. 10:39).

This is a key truth. Many want to hold on to their soul life. They want to remain in control of their lives; **they are not prepared to 'lose' their soul life by reckoning themselves dead and by submitting themselves wholeheartedly to Jesus Christ.** The endless quest for inner healing is evidence of this. Such healing is soul healing. But Jesus said that this soul life is not to be healed, it is to be lost. It is not to be the focus of attention but denied:

> If anyone would come after me, he must deny himself and take up his cross and follow me. For whoever wants to save his life will lose it, but whoever loses his life for me will find it (Matt. 16:24–5).

Notice these points from what Jesus says here:

1 **He is addressing 'anyone' who wants to follow Him,** to be a Christian.
2 **The Christian MUST deny himself,** not concentrate on himself or his healing!
3 **WHOEVER wants to save his life will lose it.** This is true for anyone.
4 **WHOEVER loses his life will find it.** Whoever submits himself to God will find what he is looking for.

So what are we looking for? Love? Joy? Peace? Of course! The qualities of patience, kindness, goodness, faithfulness, gentleness, self-control? Certainly!

Do we need God's power? Yes! Do we want to exercise His authority? We need to!

Well, none of these things is accomplished by looking at self or trying to heal self. They are all the work of God's own Spirit. **So when the soul life is submitted to the Spirit the life of God's Spirit floods through the soul, giving the believer precisely what he wants and needs.**

This is what people experience when first baptised in the Holy Spirit. Unfortunately all too often they return gradually to 'soulishness', trying to improve self instead of denying self.

SPIRIT: Love, Joy, Peace
                 Fruit of the Spirit
                 Power
                 Gifts
SOUL: Fruits and gifts of the Spirit to be expressed
                 through the soul and
BODY

Jesus makes some very extreme statements about discipleship, showing us what is involved in denying self.

If anyone comes to me and does not hate his father and mother, his wife and children, his brothers and sisters – **yes, even his own life** – he cannot be my disciple. And anyone who does not carry his cross and follow me cannot be my disciple (Luke 14:26–7).

What does it mean for a disciple to hate his own life? He is to hate it whenever his soul or self-life takes the throne instead of being submitted to God. He is to hate the very idea of his soul hindering God's purposes instead of being a vehicle to express the Holy Spirit's life. He is to hate allowing others, even those who are precious to him, to be more important than Jesus. **The Lord is to be pre-eminent at all times.**

This does not mean that he will deny his responsibilities to his family. If he is out of God's order his loved ones will suffer because of the conflicts and tensions he experiences as a result. If he is truly submitted to God, His love, joy and peace will flow through him to the benefit of those around him. God's power and authority will be able to operate in his life in the way God intends. Jesus also said:

The man who loves his life will lose it, while the man who hates his life in this world will keep it for eternal life. Whoever serves me must follow me (John 12:25–6).

The death and resurrection principle is central to the teaching and ministry of Jesus:

I tell you the truth, unless a grain of wheat falls to the ground and dies, it remains only a single seed. But if it dies, it produces many seeds (John 12:24).

The way to be fruitful is to die to self, not try to heal self!
When first baptised in the Holy Spirit it is common for believers to experience the life of the Spirit flooding their souls. They are more aware of His love than ever before; they experience His joy in greater measure. They are at peace with God in a new way; they experience the peace that passes understanding. Changes in their attitudes and behaviour take place because of the fruit the Spirit is producing in them. They are more patient, kind, faithful, etc.

The soul always wants to assert itself again, to take back control. Before being filled with the Spirit, the believer needed to submit himself to God. That submission has to be maintained if the flow of God's Spirit through the soul is to be maintained.

To return concentration to the soul, to the self, is the worst thing that could happen. Immediately the Spirit is grieved, for He cannot influence the believer in the way He desires.

This was already a problem in New Testament times. Paul asks the Galatians:

> After beginning with the Spirit, are you now trying to attain your goal by human effort? (Gal. 3:3).

I have been saddened to see so many lose their spiritual vitality and joy because they have turned in upon themselves and have become introspective, instead of radiating to others the life that was so obviously within them. I have seen churches which have experienced a significant move of God's Spirit, lose the anointing when their members become obsessed with so-called 'inner healing'.

On the other hand it is wonderful to see people change as the Holy Spirit brings them revelation that they have died with Christ, that now they are a new creation. They do not have to improve themselves or heal themselves. They have already been set free completely from their past to live the new life. So great is the power of the Truth that people are changed when they believe it!

"THE TRUTH WILL SET YOU FREE" – JESUS

Paul tells the Galatians:

> It is for freedom that Christ has set us free. Stand firm, then, and do not let yourselves be burdened again by a yoke of slavery (5:1).

THE MIND OF CHRIST

Jesus has set you free. That is an accomplished fact brought about by what He did on the cross. You do not have to return to the slavery of the past, to religious law, to soulish ways, to fleshly lusts. You are free to follow Jesus Christ, your Lord and Saviour.

Therefore, I urge you, brothers, in view of God's mercy, to offer your bodies as living sacrifices, holy and pleasing to God – this is your spiritual act of worship. Do not conform any longer to the pattern of this world, **but be transformed by the renewing of your mind.** Then you will be able to test and approve what God's will is – his good, pleasing and perfect will (Rom. 12:1–2).

The more the soul expresses the life of the Spirit, the healthier it will be and the more able to fulfil God's purpose for your life. We all recognise our need to reflect more of Jesus. **This does not happen through self-improvement, but through having the mind of Christ.**

Jesus climbed a high mountain with Peter, James and John and there He was transfigured before them. His human body became a radiant, glorious body. The Greek word 'transfigure' is used only four times in the New Testament, twice to describe this event (Matt. 17:2 and Mark 9:2); and twice to describe what God is doing in us as His children.

And we, who with unveiled faces all reflect the Lord's glory, are being transformed into his likeness with ever-increasing glory, which comes from the Lord, who is the Spirit (2 Cor. 3:18).

The word translated 'transformed' here is the same Greek word for 'transfigure'. Whereas the process for Jesus could be an instantaneous one because He lived in perfection, for us it is a gradual one. We are being 'transfigured' with ever-increasing glory! How? By our minds being renewed by the Truth:

Do not conform any longer to the pattern of this world, but be transformed by the renewing of your mind (Rom. 12:2).

You are 'transfigured' by the renewing of your mind; by your thinking coming in line with God's thinking, with His Word.

You will never be transfigured by soul-searching or soul-healing – only by faith in the Truth!

To have the mind of Christ does not mean that every thought you have comes from Him. It means that you now have the ability to think as Jesus thinks. The Holy Spirit encourages you to see yourself and others as Jesus would; to have this attitude of faith towards your circumstances.

It is only by checking your thinking with God's Word that you can determine whether you are truly thinking with the mind of Christ.

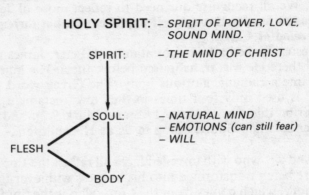

HOLY SPIRIT: – *SPIRIT OF POWER, LOVE, SOUND MIND.*

SPIRIT: – *THE MIND OF CHRIST*

SOUL: – *NATURAL MIND*
– *EMOTIONS (can still fear)*
– *WILL*

FLESH

BODY

THE BODY

Your soul is in a pivotal position between the spirit and the body. 'God is Spirit, and his worshippers must worship in spirit and in truth' (John 4:24). You have direct communion with God through your spirit. This is where revelation occurs.

Your body on the other hand is in touch with the world around you, which offers constant temptation to the senses. The body craves to be satisfied and would yield to these temptations unless kept in line by your soul.

To submit your soul to the Spirit gives you life and peace. To allow the soul to be controlled by bodily senses is spiritual death. The Holy Spirit draws your soul towards the Truth; your body is intent on pleasing self.

If you want to please God, you will ensure your soul is kept under the influence of the Holy Spirit. You have to remember that at any time your soul can deny Him instead of honouring Him. It is for this reason that Jesus said that anyone who would be His disciple would have to deny himself *day by day*.

God gives you the Truth of His Word, not to find fault with you, but to set you free. The enemy constantly accuses and tries to make you feel condemned. But Jesus died to set you free.

The more you analyse yourself, your soul life, the less likely you are to live by faith. The more your soul looks to the Lord, the more you are delivered from self.

My soul finds rest in God alone (Ps. 62:1).

God's Spirit cannot act directly on the body; He has to work through your soul. He is drawing your soul to love and obey God; your body wants you to love the world. In this life you will always know this conflict.

So you have to decide whether the supernatural or the natural is going to reign in your life. **Neither God nor the devil can do anything in you without your consent.** You are given the sovereignty of your life. You can either yield that sovereignty to God, or maintain it for yourself, which is precisely what the devil suggests you should do. He wants you to concentrate on that soul life, not 'lose' it!

SUBMIT

You have to keep your soul humble before God in order to please Him. Jesus Himself is the example of this. In His humanity He denied Himself in order to obey the will of His Father:

Your attitude should be the same as that of Christ Jesus: Who, being in very nature God, did not consider equality with God something to be grasped, but made himself nothing, taking the very nature of a servant, being made in human likeness (Phil. 2:5–7).

Your attitude should be the same, says Paul. Jesus never acted independently of His Father. This was the very thing Satan tempted Him to do in the wilderness immediately before His ministry began. What a temptation it must have been to turn stones into bread when you haven't eaten for forty days, especially if you have the power to do so! But Jesus would not even consider doing anything at the devil's instigation; He acted only in obedience to His Father's wishes. **Jesus kept His soul life in constant submission to His Father.** That was why He could always exercise authority over the enemy and all his demonic powers.

Submit yourselves, then, to God. Resist the devil, and he will flee from you (Jas. 4:7).

Many try to resist the devil without first submitting themselves to God; and then they wonder why often they seem to be defeated rather than victorious. Instead of submitting they hold on to self. Their heart cry is: 'Love *me*. Accept *me*. Let *me* know that you appreciate *me*.' A far cry from losing self!

And often well-meaning Christians help them unwittingly in their sin. They try to encourage this self-life. The truth is that of myself I am a totally unacceptable failure, unable to do anything to please God. **But in Christ I am a new creation, made righteous and totally acceptable to God through Him.**

8 Living in Love

Jesus tells His disciples to 'remain in my love' (John 15:9). You can only remain where God has already placed you: 'in Christ'. To live in Him is to live in love.

To live in God's love is not to live in emotional sentimentality, but in the One whose love is eternal, steadfast, strong and utterly reliable. Jesus's command to remain in His love follows one of His most faith-encouraging statements:

As the Father has loved me, so have I loved you (John 15:9).

By definition, God cannot do anything imperfectly or halfheartedly. Everything Jesus does He does well! (Mark 7:37). To say that He loves is to say that He loves perfectly.

This means that God loves you, and every other born-again believer, perfectly. In other words there is no one else in the world that He loves more than you, for it is impossible to improve on the perfect!

It is not a question of whether you 'feel' this love, but that you believe in your heart that God loves you perfectly.

THE FATHER'S LOVE FOR JESUS

Jesus loves His disciples in the same way that the Father loved Him. The Father loved Him perfectly; we could not expect anything less. These are some of the ways in which the Father showed His love for Jesus:

1 **Jesus enjoyed unity with the Father.** 'The Father and I are one.'
2 **He could do nothing without the Father.** 'I can do nothing of myself.'
3 **Jesus knew He could depend on His Father to work.** He had not come to do His own will but His Father's will. He knew His prayers would be answered, that when He confronted opposition, sickness or even death, He would prevail.
4 **He knew the Father had entrusted all things to Him,** a sign of the love and trust between them.
5 **And yet the Father did not allow His love for Jesus to intrude on the purpose for which He sent Him to the world.** He allowed Him to be opposed, hated, rejected, mocked and crucified.
6 **Jesus entrusted Himself to the Father, even to the point of death, expecting that He would be raised.**
7 **Jesus was totally secure in knowing who He was, where He had come from and where He was going.**

Of course there are many other ways in which the Father and Son demonstrated the love and unity between them. Each of these points is to be reflected in our lives as His disciples, because of this truth: **in exactly the same way that the Father had loved Him, so Jesus has loved us**. This is demonstrated in the experience of those first disciples and in the lives of those who follow Him faithfully today.

JESUS'S LOVE FOR YOU

1 **Because of what He has done for you on the cross, you have been reconciled to God; you are one with Him.** You live in Jesus and He in you. You live in God and He in you

(1 John 4:15). You participate in the divine nature through His very great and precious promises (2 Pet. 1:4).

2 **Just as Jesus could do nothing without the Father, so apart from Jesus you can do nothing!** (John 15:5). Through faith in Him all things become possible for you (Mark 9:23). You can do all things through Him who strengthens you.

3 **As you believe the promises of Jesus, you will live depending on Him,** as Jesus lived in dependence on His Father. He will be with you always. He will give you whatever you ask in His name. In His love He died for you to make it possible for His Spirit to live in you, thus empowering you to do the things to which He calls you.

4 Just as the Father entrusted all things to Jesus, so He has entrusted to us as His Body the commission to make disciples of all nations. **As a member of His Body, He has given you His Kingdom, His Spirit, authority over all the power of the evil one, so that you can fulfil your part in His desire for His Kingdom to come, and His will to be done on earth as in heaven.**

5 **Like Jesus, you will be hated, rejected, persecuted, mocked for your faith.** Some will even suffer torture and martyrdom. This is the inevitable cost of bringing love to a sinful and hurting world. Such suffering for the Kingdom should never cause us to question God's love, for He is with us, no matter what we suffer for His name's sake. He brings us through triumphantly.

6 **You can let yourself die, by 'losing' your soul for Jesus's sake.** You will then find your true identity in Christ. You have been crucified with Christ. Instead of fighting for the survival of the flesh, you can rejoice that Jesus has dealt the death blow to the person you once were!

7 **Every born-again believer can be totally secure in Jesus's love. He knows he has been born of the Spirit, born 'from above'. He knows the Lord is with him always, and he is sure that when he dies he will enjoy his eternal destiny with Jesus**

in heaven. Nothing in all creation, either in heaven or earth, can separate him from God's love in Christ Jesus!

You have the assurance from Jesus: I shall lose none of all that he has given me, but raise them up at the last day (John 6:39). The believer does not need to fear death!

This is total security, but has nothing to do with emotion or 'feeling' loved.

THE INSECURE

As the love of the Spirit flows from your spirit through your soul, that love is bound on occasions to touch your emotions. But this is not 'soul-love', born of emotion; it is that which comes from the Spirit touching your emotions. And the nature of these two kinds of love is very different.

The same is true with joy and other aspects of the Holy Spirit's life within you. As this joy flows through your soul, you will sometimes 'feel' that joy and your body will want to express that joy. But this is not emotional joy. When Paul says: 'Rejoice in the Lord always', he is pointing out that at all times your focus needs to be on Jesus, no matter what our feelings or circumstances. This means that there will be many occasions when you will need to rejoice in Him as an act of the will, yet you could not feel less like rejoicing! You decide to turn away from your circumstances and feelings, focus on Jesus and rejoice in Him.

Soul-centred or self-centred Christians rarely rejoice and constantly doubt God's love for them. Many will claim they are unable to do otherwise. Once someone is born again and made one with Jesus, this certainly is not true! Nothing can separate a believer from God's love in Christ; but if he does not believe that he is loved, he will not see his need to rejoice. It is not healing he needs, but faith.

Soul-centred people concentrate on feelings. They are the ones who only believe they are loved if they *feel* loved. They believe the devil's lie that they are being hypocritical to rejoice in the Lord and praise Him when they do not feel like doing so!

In such people there is a craving to be loved, accepted, appreciated, wanted. They constantly seek encouragement and easily become dependent on ministry from others. It seems that their continual cry is: 'Love me, love me. Please tell me that you love me, that you really appreciate me.' Assurances of your love, or even of God's love mean very little. Such assurances have a short-term effect; it is not long before they want further assurances that they are loved.

This is no way for a Christian to live, with a basic insecurity, doubting they are loved, accepted and appreciated by the Lord and by others. However, the answer is not to minister to the insecurity by examining it, seeking to find the reason for it. **Their basic problem is one of unbelief, for it is only faith in God's love for them that can truly heal them of the insecurity. And faith NEVER comes from examining yourself, only through a revelation of the Truth, by hearing God's Word!**

It is the Truth, and only the Truth, that can set a person free from insecurity and self-doubt, giving him the assurance that God has loved him in Christ.

The truth will show him that God has declared His love for him in Jesus. It is only as he loses self, submitting his soul to God, that the love of the Spirit will flood his soul. It is only as he believes in the power of Jesus's blood that he will know he is accepted in the beloved, that he is already made totally righteous in God's sight. And if he is accepted by God he then can begin to find a new security in his inter-personal relationships.

He will know he is appreciated as he sees the fruit produced by the Holy Spirit's activity flowing through him. He will discover that God is able to use him; he is not a useless reject!

Once again it must be emphasised that the answer of the New Testament is not to concentrate on the soul by seeking to heal the soul. Insecure people are already too self-centred. **Concentrating on the self-life will only encourage them to be more so, and will give them the impression that the answer to their need is in themselves and not in Christ.**

Every need has been met in Jesus. Those who imagine they must be totally outside of God's love can only come into a true awareness of His love and acceptance through revelation of the Truth in their hearts. Then the Holy Spirit will saturate their souls with His *agape* love, so different from the soul-love based on emotion. As they obey Jesus and 'lose' their souls, they find the true love they need, a love that will never change with circumstances, a love that enfolds them eternally. A love that is expressed in positive action rather than emotion; and yet a love that satisfies emotional need when it is allowed to flood the soul.

The more anyone becomes abandoned to God's love, the more secure in that love he becomes, conscious that no matter what the feelings, problems, circumstances, opposition or suffering, nothing can separate him from God's love. His security comes from his faith in that love, quite apart from whether he feels His love or joy!

LOVING OBEDIENCE

The importance of knowing God's love, though, is not to give us security but to enable obedience to the Lord. It is through obedience that the believer will remain in His love:

> If you obey my commands, you will remain in my love, just as I have obeyed my Father's commands and remain in his love. I have told you this so that my joy may be in you and that your joy may be complete (John 15:10–11).

The soul-centred Christian becomes so wrapped up in his self-concern that he loses sight of his need of obedience. He *feels* unable to obey, to reach out to others in love.

It is not the self-centred soul life that God loves. He loves the new creation this believer has become, the one who is in Christ and in whom Christ lives. He loves this one that is totally accepted in His beloved Son.

There is a danger of encouraging people to believe that God loves what He does not love. He definitely does not love soulish self-centredness. The soul life of every believer is in the process of being sanctified with ever-increasing glory, as the believer submits himself to the Holy Spirit and the Word of God.

It is obedience to 'lose' your soul life; disobedience to concentrate on that life. **The only way to obey Jesus is to do what He says.** And He has made it clear that *anyone* who would be His disciple must deny self and take up his cross daily – irrespective of who he is, or what problems or needs he has! ANYONE means ANYONE.

It is not for us to turn round to Jesus and tell Him He was wrong. We would invite a similar rebuke to the one Peter received for disagreeing with what Jesus said: 'Get behind me, Satan!' . . . 'you do not have in mind the things of God, but the things of men' (Matt. 16:23).

You abide in Jesus's love by submitting yourself to God's will, walking in His truth, and living in the fullness of His joy.

When we seek any other way than His way, there are inevitable tensions between God and ourselves. The Holy Spirit within the believer, on the other hand, encourages a sense of peace, well-being and fulfilment whenever he does what God wants.

The world craves after self-fulfilment. Jesus's answer to this is to tell us to 'lose' self and then we will find true fulfilment. To concentrate on self is in direct opposition to 'losing' self!

God has put His love into the believer so that this love can flow out of him as a river of living water. He defeats his own ends if he sits around waiting to be loved instead of seeking to love others by giving to them. For we are to love others in the same way that Jesus loves us!

ANXIETY

Some consider this impossible because they feel so burdened by anxiety. Paul tells us:

Do not be anxious about anything, but in everything, by prayer and petition, with thanksgiving, present your requests to God. And the peace of God, which transcends all understanding, will guard your hearts and your minds in Christ Jesus (Phil. 4:6–7).

Paul does not suggest a person should examine the cause of his anxieties. Instead he tells him to turn to God:

1 **You are not to be anxious about anything.** This only endorses what Jesus said: 'Do not worry about your life' (Matt. 6:25). This is a command from God, and you are able to do whatever He commands you.
2 **In every situation you are to pray.**
3 **You are presenting your requests to God,** not man.
4 **You are to pray with thanksgiving** because the Father will answer the prayer of faith. There will be times when you need to persevere in prayer until you know you are genuinely thankful. Many are defeated because they do not pray through in this way. Instead of being thankful they resent their circumstances.
5 **When you pray with thanksgiving, God's peace will descend on you.**
6 **This peace is beyond understanding.**
7 **It will guard your heart (spirit) and mind (soul) in Christ Jesus.** You will be able to cope, no matter how desperate your circumstances may seem.

This is a far cry from those who seek to minister into people's anxieties by substituting something completely different from what we read in God's Word. It is by turning to God that a person will be lifted up:

Come near to God and he will come near to you . . . Humble yourselves before the Lord, and he will lift you up (Jas. 4:8,10).

God wants every believer to develop his own relationship with Himself, and this is done by personal faith in His Word and prayer. **The only way to learn how to pray is to pray!** Jesus said:

Therefore do not worry about tomorrow, for tomorrow will worry about itself. Each day has enough trouble of its own (Matt. 6:34).

The Lord knows about the circumstances each of His children has to face. He will never allow any to be tempted beyond what he is able to endure (1 Cor. 10:13); **neither will He allow him to be overcome by events.**

In His sovereign overruling of your life, He ensures that you will have enough to cope with on each day. If you take tomorrow's burden on yourself as well as today's load, you will be overburdened. It is then that you will feel you cannot cope.

You feel overcome by events when you try to deal with today, tomorrow and the possible problems of the future all at once! This is not the way Jesus tells you to order your life.

Many disobey what He says, and then blame Him for the consequences. If we only obey Him we will find that in His love He cares for us, enables us, sustains us in every difficulty, will not allow us to fall and will lead us in victory!

9 Faith

The righteous will live by faith – not counselling! They put their faith in God daily. They trust in what He says and in what He has done for them, so that He will impact their lives in practical ways. They realise that faith is more than believing a series of doctrinal statements about God. It is putting their complete trust in the One of whom the Bible speaks.

When Jesus dealt with individuals who came to Him for help, He asked questions to see if they believed He would do what they asked. He often made it clear that their faith was the cause of their healing:

'Go! **It will be done just as you believed it would'.** And his servant was healed at that very hour (Matt. 8:13).

She said to herself, 'If I only touch his cloak, I will be healed.' Jesus turned and saw her. 'Take heart, daughter,' he said, **'your faith has healed you.'** And the woman was healed from that moment (Matt. 9:21–2).

Then he touched their eyes and said, **'According to your faith will it be done to you'** (Matt. 9:29).

Then Jesus answered, **'Woman, you have great faith!** Your

request is granted.' And her daughter was healed from that very hour (Matt. 15:28).

When Jesus saw their faith, he said to the paralytic, 'Son, your sins are forgiven' (Mark 2:5).

Then he said to him, 'Rise and go; **your faith has made you well'** (Luke 17:19).

Jesus said to the woman, **'Your faith has saved you;** go in peace' (Luke 7:50).

I have heard people try to explain away this concentration on faith; they claim that Jesus didn't really mean that faith can heal! Then why did He say so? Jesus was certainly capable of saying what He meant! He chose to say, 'Your faith has healed you,' because that is precisely what He meant.

This demonstrates the great power that faith in Jesus brings into a believer's life. It is the voice of Truth who said: 'It will be done just as you believed it would,' and, 'According to your faith will it be done for you.'

It seems that only when people were so demonically bound did Jesus not look for a response of faith until after the healing. (Although even Legion, who had two thousand demons, came and fell at the feet of Jesus begging for help!)

No matter what the cause, faith in Him was enough to produce healing. Sometimes, as in the case of the paralytic who was let down through the roof, sin may have been either the cause of the sickness or a hindrance to receiving the healing. But sin could easily be dealt with by the forgiveness Jesus offered.

UNBELIEF

When Jesus first appeared to the Eleven in His risen body 'he rebuked them for their lack of faith and their stubborn refusal to believe those who had seen him after he had risen' (Mark 16:14).

Just as faith is very powerful in a positive sense, so is unbelief in a negative way. Jesus seemed to be disappointed, and even frustrated with His disciples when they failed to act in faith. For example, when He came down from the Mount of Transfiguration, He said to the nine disciples who had failed to heal the epileptic boy:

O unbelieving and perverse generation . . . how long shall I stay with you? How long shall I put up with you? Bring the boy here to me (Matt. 17:17).

Not the most encouraging thing He ever said! But He wanted to shake them out of their unbelief. He emphasised to them afterwards that they had not been able to drive out the demon, 'because you have so little faith' (Matt. 17:20).

Jesus made it clear that **'Everything is possible for him who believes'** (Mark 9:23). Yet in Nazareth, 'He could not do any miracles there, except lay his hands on a few sick people and heal them. **And he was amazed at their lack of faith'** (Mark 6:5–6).

Faith is a choice. You have to decide whether to believe what God says in His Word, or those things which oppose faith. There are five main opponents to faith which we must mention briefly:

1 **REASON** – your natural, rational, reasoning power. Reason will limit God, because reason is natural, not supernatural. As you submit your mind to the influence of God's Spirit, He will guide you into the truth of God's Word, which is supernatural truth. This will not limit your thinking abilities but will expand your mind. **You will think with the mind of Christ. You will see the supernatural possibilities because you have all the resources of God's Spirit and Kingdom available to you.** For this reason you are urged to 'set your mind on things above' (Col. 3:2).

2 **EMOTIONS** – It is often much easier to believe feelings than God's Word. But feelings are unreliable and change

readily from moment to moment, often in relation to your thinking or the circumstances in which you are placed. The truth, on the other hand, never changes. 'Heaven and earth will pass away, but my words will never pass away' (Matt. 24:35). Truth is eternal. **Believing the Truth will change your feelings. Believing your feelings will often cause you to deny the Truth!**

Like reason, your emotions are given you by God; so they are important. The soul, including the emotional side of your life, is to be the servant of the Spirit. God wants you to express His love, joy and peace; not believe the negative self-centred emotions which contradict His purposes.

These negative emotions dominate some people's lives, which is evidence that they need the mind of Christ. It is only by believing you are who God says you are that you will have victory in the emotions.

3 **CIRCUMSTANCES** – These too are often negative. Jesus does not promise us an easy life. 'In the world you will have tribulation,' He says – and everyone believes that! However, He teaches us to approach our circumstances with faith, to speak to 'mountains' and command them to move. He gives believers authority to bind and loose, to prevent or permit on earth **whatever** is prevented or permitted in heaven (Matt. 18:18). They are not to accept them with a resignation that suggests God wants them to be stuck with these problems.

Circumstances are not to rule you; you are to learn how to exercise faith and so overcome your circumstances.

You have to choose whether to believe the facts or the Truth, which is able to change the facts. You have to make your choice in each situation!

4 **SATAN** – The enemy does not want you to act with faith, or to exercise the authority you have as a believer; so he appeals to your reason. 'Be reasonable', is typical of his suggestions. He also appeals to negative feelings, encouraging you to concentrate on yourself and your circumstances rather than on Jesus and God's Word.

His aim is to tempt you to concentrate on self, to encourage you to soulishness and so prevent you from walking in the Spirit.

The devil is the deceiver. He tries to deceive by suggesting you will be freed from your problems by concentrating on healing your self-life. He wants you to concentrate on self rather than 'lose' your soul as Jesus instructs you. **He wants you to believe you are in bondage to your past, instead of recognising that you have died and are now set free to live the new life.**

God does not condemn us even when we have been deceived. A person is only deceived when he firmly believes he is right, but isn't. It is deception to think that we will be set free by practices claimed to be 'consistent with the truth'. What is wrong or inadequate with the Truth itself? Jesus says that the truth will set us free, not something that is claimed to be akin to the truth! Often the things which are said to be 'consistent with the truth' are a subtle denial of the Truth. The enemy can appear as an angel of light!

The devil is also the accuser of the brethren. He attempts to make them feel condemned and so disbelieve what God has done for them in Christ. He wants to steal, kill and destroy. He will try to steal the Truth from you because he knows that he is overcome when you operate in faith in God's Word. He cannot undo what God has done for you; he can only try to encourage you to disbelieve it! Accusation is an effective way of doing this. 'You are a failure', 'You are no good', 'Call yourself a Christian?', 'Look at yourself!', 'How could God love you?'

Never listen to his lies. Listen to the Truth!

5 **TRADITION** – Many fail to realise how their church traditions often contradict the Truth. Jesus warned the disciples: 'Be on your guard against the yeast of the Pharisees and Sadducees' (Matt. 16:6).

A little yeast affects the whole batch of dough. The disciples came to realise that Jesus was warning them against the teaching of these religious groups. Jesus warned:

You have let go of the commands of God and are holding on to the traditions of men (Mark 7:8).

And He pointed out the devastating consequences of this:

Thus you nullify the word of God by your tradition that you have handed down. And you do many things like that (v. 13).

God calls every believer to live by faith in His Word, not traditions which nullify His Word!

Without faith it is impossible to please God (Heb. 11:6).

Everything that does not come from faith is sin (Rom. 14:23).

And that includes traditions!

BEING SURE

No wonder, with all these things opposing faith, that Paul speaks about fighting the good fight of faith. It will certainly be a fight, but a victorious one!

The nearest the New Testament comes to a definition of faith is in the well-known verse of Hebrews 11:1.

Now faith is being sure of what we hope for and certain of what we do not see.

Notice that faith is not trying to believe something that is impossible to believe. It is being *sure* and *certain*. **You are only in a position of faith concerning those things about which you are sure and certain.**

In all probability you are sitting in a chair as you read this. Before sitting down, you did not stand over the chair saying: 'I believe this chair will take my weight. I believe it. I really believe it. This chair will take my weight.' You were so sure and certain that it would support you that you sat down without giving the matter a thought. (No doubt someone, somewhere, will be sitting on a rickety chair that inspired doubt and challenged faith!)

If I were to say to you: 'Jesus is Lord! Do you believe that?' you would immediately say 'Yes', if you are a born-again Christian. You would not need to deliberate or think about your answer. You know He is Lord. You are sure and certain about this.

God wants you to be as sure and certain about everything He says in His Word, including all the things He has done for you and all He says about you.

He wants you to be sure and certain that you have died and your life is now hidden with Christ in God. He wants you to be sure and certain that you have been crucified with Christ, that you no longer live but Christ lives in you.

He wants you to be sure and certain that you have 'lost' your life, your soul, that you have submitted yourself to the authority of Jesus and the rule of His Spirit in your life.

He wants you to believe, to be sure and certain, that the old has gone and the new has come; that you are a new creation. He wants you to be sure and certain that He has blessed you in Christ with every spiritual blessing in heaven, that you have fullness of life in Him, that He will meet every need of yours according to His riches in glory in Christ Jesus.

Paul says: 'The only thing that counts is faith expressing itself through love' (Gal. 5:6).

You are not sure and certain of these things if you are trying to crucify yourself, fight yourself, heal yourself. In which case you need to ask the Holy Spirit to give you revelation of these truths so that they live in your spirit.

OLD OR NEW

The following shows two possible scenarios for a person's life.
You belong to either one column or the other. **You cannot
belong to both.** You have to decide whether you belong to the
old or the new!

OLD	*NEW*
A sinner	A saint
Belong to Kingdom of darkness	Belong to Kingdom of God
Bound by sin	Set free from sin
Condemned	Forgiven
Unrighteous	Made righteous
Unredeemed	Redeemed
Unholy	Holy in Christ
Satan your father	God your Father
Child of darkness	Child of Light
Victim of your old nature	A new nature: Christ in you
Fallen	New creation
No eternal inheritance	Co-heir with Christ
Unworthy	Made worthy
Unacceptable	Accepted in Christ
No glory	Already glorified
No place in heaven	Seated in heavenly places
Without God's power	Filled with power through the Holy Spirit
Sick	Healed by His stripes
A failure	God's child
Ruled by law of sin and death	Ruled by Spirit of life
Spirit of fear	Spirit of power, love and sound mind

What a contrast! And remember you cannot belong to both
sides. **If you belong to Jesus Christ everything in the right-hand**

column is true for you: everything. It may be tempting to think of yourself as being partly in both columns, but this is only because you don't share God's perspective on your life!

Many seek 'counsel' because they see themselves on the wrong side of the line. It is fatal to minister to them as if they are right in that assessment. They are only in the left-hand column if they are not yet born again.

We shall see later that some very broken people have to go through a process of conversion to be rescued from the old and brought into the Truth. But once they have reached the point of new birth they are made new and *everything* in the right-hand column is true about them whether they realise this or not!

Satan wants the Christian to disbelieve what God has done for him. He is powerless to undo God's work; so he tries to entice the Christian to believe he is still bound by the past, and therefore unable to live in the good of his new life in Christ. **Satan is a liar and the father of all lies.** Going back into the old can never liberate a person and make it possible to live the new life. That can only be lived by faith in Jesus. It is a lie to suggest I can only live the new if I dig and delve into the old. **The old has gone, crucified with Christ. It has already been dealt with. I have already been set free from my past by what He has done. Faith accepts what He has done for me.**

Nothing can be added to the finished work of the cross. Paul wrote the letter to the Galatians in white-hot anger. He had preached the good news of the cross to the Galatian church. But he was followed around by other preachers who suggested that faith in what Jesus had done was insufficient for salvation. To this needed to be added observance of the law, including circumcision for Gentile believers.

Paul was livid and suggested that the Galatians must be under some kind of curse to believe such a thing. What made Paul so angry?

The suggestion of these other preachers undermined the whole cause of the Gospel, suggesting that faith in Jesus and what He did on the cross, was insufficient for complete salvation. Such an impression is often given today. To the initial response of faith in Christ some seem to suggest must be added counselling, inner healing or healing of the memories! Paul would be equally livid if he were ministering today. He would not be able to understand how believers could be so deceived.

He asked the Galatians whether they had received the Holy Spirit and seen God working miracles among them through observing the law, or by believing what they had heard of the truth as he had proclaimed it. His questions could have only one answer: by believing what they heard!

The same is true today. The only way to freedom is by believing what we hear in God's Word about the finished and complete work of salvation accomplished on the cross. In that act everything was accomplished for your total well-being in spirit, soul and body.

Faith reckons Jesus's death as your death; His resurrection as your resurrection. The one who is accepted in Christ becomes as acceptable to God as Christ. He is made whole by what He has already done.

PART 2

COUNSELLING OTHERS WITH THE TRUTH

10   Anointed by the Spirit

Any counsellor needs to be completely dependent on the Holy Spirit, the Counsellor God has given us. It is *His* truth we are to give, not our own advice! And He directs us to Jesus. So our real task is to show believers they are able to look directly to the Lord for leading and guidance, for help or healing. The Holy Spirit lives within them to reveal the Truth of Jesus to them and so enable them to walk in freedom in the power of God.

BORN AGAIN

When seeking to help others, it is first essential to ensure that they have been born again. This may seem obvious, but this is by no means the case. To be born again a person has to come to repentance and faith in Jesus Christ and all He has done on the cross.

Many today are not 'birthed' properly. They have been asked to make a sincere, but often superficial, response to the Gospel. It is common to hear people use such phrases as: 'He has made a commitment'; or 'She has asked Jesus into her heart'.

Both these phrases are non-scriptural and do not necessarily mean that the person has either repented, or put his or her faith in Jesus Christ crucified and risen.

Over the years many people with major problems have been referred to us by churches all over the nation and beyond. It has been amazing how it has been assumed by those ministering to them that they were born again, yet this sadly is often not the case. We have needed to lead them to repentance and faith and into a personal relationship with Jesus. So first they needed to hear the good news of what Jesus has done for them on the cross.

It is unwise to take it for granted that a person understands the cross, simply because he goes to church! Many do not know that they have been crucified with Christ.

The sad thing is that many of those referred to us have been subjected to prolonged ministry by those who have *assumed* they are born again, simply because they have made 'commitments' or attend church services. Frequently we find that they have never been confronted with the need to repent. On more than one occasion people have said to me: 'Why should I repent? I'm an Anglican!'

It goes without saying that church affiliation is no passport to heaven – **only the new birth, following repentance and faith.**

Bringing someone to repentance, faith in Jesus and new birth will itself resolve many issues in his or her life. In addition, the believer needs to be baptised in the Holy Spirit, for then the life of the Spirit will infuse his or her soul. This again will resolve many issues, for such an event leads to a great awareness of the Lord's presence in the believer's life.

Worship becomes more meaningful for he now knows the One to whom he prays. He experiences the life of Jesus flowing through him and out of him as never before. Love and joy fill his soul and he knows God's peace, in a new way. There is a great increase in the fruit of the Spirit in his life and he will soon find he can use the gifts of the Spirit, if encouraged to do so.

This, of course, does not herald the end of all his dilemmas. The life of the Spirit needs to continue to infuse his soul. **He needs not only to be baptised in the Holy Spirit, but to live submerged in the Spirit.** Paul tells the Ephesians to continue to be filled with the Holy Spirit. This needs to be a continual process that begins with a definite event performed by Jesus Himself!

BAPTISM IN THE HOLY SPIRIT

We have seen that at the point of new birth the Holy Spirit brings life to the human spirit of the new believer. We have seen also the need for every Christian to continue to submit his soul and body to the Lord so that the life of the Holy Spirit can flow through him and out of him as rivers of living water.

Jesus is the Baptiser in the Holy Spirit:

He will baptise you with the Holy Spirit and with fire (Matt. 3:11).

To baptise is to immerse, to infuse completely. When a person is baptised in water his body is immersed to indicate that his old life is dead and lays buried with Christ. He arises out of the water to live the new life in Christ.

When he is baptised in the Spirit his soul is 'immersed' in the Spirit. The life of the Holy Spirit floods through his soul, empowering him to live his new life in Christ. Jesus said:

You will receive power when the Holy Spirit comes on you; and you will be my witnesses . . . (Acts 1:8).

Water baptism signifies the person has been incorporated by faith into Christ. **Baptism in the Holy Spirit empowers him to live in Christ.**

Water baptism is into Christ. **Baptism in the Holy Spirit is given to the individual believer by Christ Himself** in fulfilment of His promise.

It goes without saying, therefore, that these two events should not be confused; both are intended by God for every believer! In some cases the two events may happen consecutively on the same day, as with Jesus. He submitted Himself to be baptised by John the Baptist; but the Holy Spirit came on Him when He came up out of the water – not while He was in it!

> As soon as Jesus was baptised, he went up out of the water. At that moment heaven was opened, and he saw the Spirit of God descending like a dove and lighting on him. And a voice from heaven said, 'This is my Son, whom I love; with him I am well pleased' (Matt. 3:16–17).

For others, the two events are separated by several years, not because this is God's intention, but usually because the believer has not been taught that a baptism in the Holy Spirit is available and necessary for him.

Often people are perplexed as to why they are not baptised in the Holy Spirit. Usually they think this is the case because they have not spoken in tongues. They are putting the cart before the horse. You do not speak in tongues in order to be filled with the Spirit, but because you have been filled! The baptism comes first, and this is a promise from God to be appropriated by faith, and then the tongue! Jesus says:

> Ask and it will be given to you . . . everyone who asks receives . . . how much more will your Father in heaven give the Holy Spirit to those who ask him! (Luke 11:9–13).

If the person has already received prayer to be baptised in the Holy Spirit on a number of occasions, I point out that it is not more prayer he needs, but faith that God has honoured His promise! **Once people believe they have received they will have no difficulty in speaking in tongues.**

Once again we see how people are prone to exalt experience above God's Word. When we believe the Word we enter into the necessary experience. (This is not to say that on occasions there may be some other reason for a person not receiving. In practice, though, I have found this to be rarely the case.)

It is common for the person's whole demeanour to change

when he suddenly realises that God has already given him the blessing. 'You mean, *I am* baptised in the Spirit?' they often ask. When assured of God's faithfulness many have prayed in tongues there and then, without receiving any further ministry!

Once again this shows the power over the individual of unbelief and faith. It is tragic when this has not been discerned by pastors or counsellors, who suggest there must be some moral reason why God has withheld the blessing. This only confirms the person's own worst fears and leads to intensive introspective soul-searching, which does nothing to encourage faith!

ANOINTED

But you have an anointing from the Holy One, and all of you know the truth (1 John 2:20).

This is true for every born-again believer. John then points out the implication of having such an anointing:

As for you, the anointing you received from him remains in you, and you do not need anyone to teach you. But as his anointing teaches you about all things and as that anointing is real, not counterfeit – just as it has taught you, remain in him (1 John 2:27).

Consider these points:

1 **The believer has 'an anointing'.** This does not mean that he should refrain from seeking further anointing, but it does indicate that he has already received an anointing.
2 **This anointing comes from God, the Holy One.** He anoints the believer with His own Spirit, the Holy Spirit.
3 **This anointing enables all who receive it to know the Truth.** The Spirit of truth will reveal Jesus, the Truth, and His words of truth to the believer.

4 **This anointing remains in you as a believer.** God does not take it away. He knows you need constant revelation of the Truth.

5 **Because of this anointing you don't need anyone to teach you.** You don't need to use anyone else as a substitute for the Holy Spirit. He will bring you the Word you need in every situation. He will be your Helper, your personal Counsellor.

Obviously John does not mean that you would never need to be taught the Gospel. 'Teacher' is one of the God-given ministries to the Church (1 Cor. 12:28). In this context John is saying:

> See that what you have heard from the beginning remains in you. If it does, you also will remain in the Son and in the Father (1 John 2:24).

The Holy Spirit reminds us of what we have been taught. We are to look to Him for His counsel. God has given you the anointing to do this.

6 **This anointing will teach you about all things.** You have the Teacher within you. He will point you, not back to your past nor inwards to yourself, but to the aspect of God's truth you need at any particular time.

It is no excuse to say that you do not hear the Lord's voice clearly. Jesus said that His sheep know His voice. He knows you. He knows what to say to you and how to say it. You hear His voice, but may on occasions push His words away because you don't like what He is saying!

7 **This anointing is real, not counterfeit.** The Holy Spirit will never lead you into deception, or into anything which contradicts God's Word.

8 **This anointing teaches you to remain in Jesus,** to live in Him. He said:

> If you remain in me and my words remain in you, ask whatever you wish, and it will be given you (John 15:7).

What greater promise could you want? 'Whatever you wish!' This is true, not only for you but for any Christian who turns to you for help.

If he does not allow Jesus's words to live in him what are you to do? Certainly not substitute something else for His commands! The Holy Spirit will give you the right words to say to that person at that time. You speak in the name of Jesus; so you will say what He would say in that situation. You would do better to remain silent if you are not prepared to speak the Truth in love.

Peter at Caesarea Philippi had to face the uncomfortable fact that not everything he said was the truth. One minute he was speaking revelation from the Father in heaven; the next he was contradicting Jesus and being told he was Satan's mouthpiece!

The lesson to learn from this is never to contradict the Truth! Why contradict what can set you and others free? To disagree with the Truth is to remain in bondage or even make the situation worse!

If anyone speaks, he should do it as one speaking the very words of God. If anyone serves, he should do it with the strength God provides, so that in all things God may be praised through Jesus Christ (1 Pet. 4:11).

When you speak a word from God into people's lives, things will happen to them. Life or healing can be imparted to them by the Lord. Paul says:

For in him you have been enriched in every way – in all your speaking and in all your knowledge. **Therefore you do not lack any spiritual gift** as you eagerly wait for our Lord Jesus Christ to be revealed (1 Cor. 1:5,7).

This is true for you as you counsel others; it is also true for those you counsel. Paul is speaking about every believer, 'all

those everywhere who call on the name of our Lord Jesus
Christ – their Lord and ours' (v. 2).

In Christ, every believer has been enriched in every way. He
may not know or believe this. He almost certainly won't *feel* it.
Nevertheless this is the Truth.

How could anything less be the Truth if he lives in God and
God in him? He has been enriched in his speech, which means
that he is able to agree with the Truth and speak it over his
own life and circumstances. He has been enriched in all his
knowledge, meaning, of course, knowledge of the Truth!

I need to repeat time and time again, that you will find what
a person needs is not someone else to pray with him, but
someone to direct him to the Truth. This was Paul's intention
when penning his epistles to different churches. For the most
part he is not bringing his readers fresh revelation, but
reminding them of what they had already been taught. He
regularly used such phrases as 'You know that . . .', 'We know
that . . .'. He points them again and again to Jesus and to what
He has done for them.

All the gifts of the Holy Spirit are available for you to use.
And the Holy Spirit is within to help every Spirit-filled believer
in his need. However, you want to help him hear the Lord for
himself and to realise these spiritual gifts are his too. He has
his own anointing from the Holy One and needs to flow in the
anointing.

It is all too common for believers to experience a baptism in
the Holy Spirit that transforms their Christian lives – but only
for a few weeks. During that time they know considerable
victory over their problems because they are so aware of Jesus
and His love. But slowly they return to soulishness; they take
their eyes off Him and back on to themselves and their
circumstances. Then instead of overcoming their problems
they feel overcome by them!

For a while their souls were submitted to God but slowly
their self-life reasserted itself, and it seemed that the blessing of
the Spirit diminished.

That is how it seems experientially; but God has not taken anything away from the believer. He simply is no longer living in the full good of what God has given him. So it is important to:

1 **ensure that the person is born again**
2 **ensure he has been baptised in the Holy Spirit**
3 **ensure that he is living submerged in the Spirit.** In other words, he is walking in the Spirit, seeking to live in obedience to Jesus.

It will prove to be a self-defeating process to try and counsel people while ignoring any of these three essential elements in any believer's response to the Gospel. Without his desire for all three, any help you can give him will be severely limited.

The Holy Spirit is the only one who can live fully the teaching of Jesus. **He does this in the lives of believers who are prepared to co-operate with Him.** Nobody can live the Christian life in his own strength or by his own efforts. He will either experience constant failure, or will construct a legalistic cage for himself.

God's perspective on a person's life is often totally different from his own perspective. The Christian sees a problem or series of problems that he wants God to deal with; **the Lord sees someone He loves, who needs to draw near to Him and to live in the Spirit.**

THE MINISTRY OF THE HOLY SPIRIT

The Holy Spirit living within the believer has a ministry to that person. **The one seeking to help needs to co-operate with this ministry, not replace it.** It is not his own spiritual expertise that will stand the person in good stead in the years ahead, but the believer's own relationship with His Spirit. The counsellor may be able to help in some way to establish the person more firmly in that relationship; but from the beginning his purpose is to direct the person to Jesus not to himself for ministry!

The Holy Spirit has a number of important functions to perform in the believer. The following is only a selection of these:

1 **He is the Spirit of truth, who will guide the believer to the Truth: God's Word** (John 16:13).

2 **He will remind the believer of all that Jesus has done for him or her** (John 14:26).

3 **'The Spirit helps us in our weakness'** (Rom. 8:26).

4 **The Holy Spirit is given to help us in prayer.** Scripture says: 'Pray in the Spirit on all occasions' (Eph. 6:18). This will involve the gift of tongues, available to all Spirit-filled believers.

5 **He who speaks in a tongue edifies himself,** builds himself up – the very thing needed by the one seeking help (1 Cor. 14:4)

6 **He who speaks in a tongue speaks to God** (1 Cor. 14:2). The Holy Spirit within will pray to the Father for the person in precisely the right way. He always knows what to pray; and you can be sure the Father listens to the voice of His own Spirit.

7 **The Holy Spirit intercedes for us** (Rom. 8:26).

8 **The Holy Spirit wants the controlling interest in the Christian's life.** He wants to lead and guide him, but will only work with his co-operation. He will never force the believer to respond.

9 **The Holy Spirit 'will not speak on his own; he will speak only what he hears'** (John 16:13). What the Spirit says is what the Father says to the believer.

10 **'He will bring glory to me by taking from what is mine and making it known to you'** (John 16:14). He will reveal Jesus to the believer.

11 **He will empower the believer to do whatever God asks of him.** So it is never true for a Christian to say: 'I can't' – if he trusts himself to the Holy Spirit working in and through him.

12 **The believer does not lack any spiritual gift** (1 Cor. 1:7). All are available to him. In 1 Corinthians 12, Paul is talking about the use of the gifts in a public context, 'for the common good'. In worship, not everybody is to exercise all of the gifts on every occasion! The Holy Spirit gives 'to each' a particular manifestation of the Spirit. So this does indicate that everyone present is expected to use the gifts!

The public use of gifts is to be exercised in an orderly fashion. But this does not mean that a believer can only ever expect to manifest one gift. All the gifts are available to him all of the time for his personal use, as and when he needs to make use of them, which is often!

There is little point in God providing these gifts to help the believer, if he or she either ignores them or never learns to use them!

13 **The believer should 'eagerly desire spiritual gifts'** (1 Cor. 14:1). In other words, to use what God has made available to him. Paul sees no competition between love and gifts. The Christian is not to live either a life of love or use the gifts. He expects both: **the gifts to be used in love.**

To desire gifts eagerly is not to say, 'Lord, I'll have this if you want to give it to me.' It is to long for the gift, plead for it to be manifested in the Christian's life.

It is obvious, therefore, that counsellors are to help believers to function more effectively in the power of the Spirit. In doing this they need to use all the Spirit's resources themselves. For He gives wisdom as to what to say and how to say it. Hours of fruitless conversation can be prevented by using the words of knowledge and wisdom the Holy Spirit gives.

The counsellor needs to avoid any pride in the use of the 'things' of the Spirit. He is not to show off his spiritual expertise, but to encourage the believer to hear God for himself!

11   The Authority of God's Word

AS MUCH AS YOU WANT

Jesus journeyed secretly to Tyre, but 'he could not keep his presence secret' (Mark 7:24).

A Gentile woman whose little daughter was possessed by an evil spirit, sought Him out in her desperation. She begged Jesus to drive out the demon. He told her:

> First let the children eat all they want, for it is not right to take the children's bread and toss it to their dogs (v. 27).

I used to have great problems with this verse, for it seems that Jesus is calling the woman a dog! What is even more remarkable is that instead of being offended, the woman agrees with Him.

> 'Yes, Lord', she replied, 'but even the dogs under the table eat the children's crumbs' (v. 28).

Jesus commended the woman for her great faith and told her that the demon had left her daughter.

Why should Jesus admire her faith? She knew she did not

have a place at His table; she was only a Gentile 'dog' with no right to make any claims upon Him. But she believed that just one crumb from that table would be sufficient for her daughter to be healed.

Look at Jesus's first words in response to the woman's request:

First, let the children eat all they want.

If a crumb could secure the healing of her daughter, what could the whole meal do for the children, who have the right to sit at the table and eat 'all they want'?

Every born-again believer is a child of God who has his or her place at the table. He can eat as much as he wants – but you cannot eat for him!

Every Christian has as much of Jesus in his life as he chooses. He spends as much time in prayer, with the Word, in worship, in fellowship, in ministry, in witnessing, as he chooses.

Encourage others to feast on the truth. One crumb healed the girl. What impact can the whole feast have on a person's life? **We can lead people to the table but we cannot force them to eat!**

Jesus issued an invitation to *all* who were wearied or burdened: **'Come to me,'** He said **'and I will give you rest.'** He didn't tell people to go to the pastor, the minister, priest or counsellor. He said: **'Come to me'.** That is still His invitation.

There will be those who will need help in coming to Jesus, the spiritually immature, those who need to be taught the truth and receive revelation of all that God has done for them. However, it is important that they should genuinely desire to follow Jesus, to be disciples, to honour Him as Lord and King.

Unfortunately, many today want to use another as an intermediary between God and themselves. They are so insecure in their own faith and relationship with God, they use someone else as a substitute for Him. They approach a man or woman instead of coming directly to Jesus.

A woman visited her pastor and for an hour poured out a

long tale of woe concerning all her problems. A famous evangelist was visiting the church and walked into the pastor's study. The pastor thought he would avail himself of the famous man's wisdom and experience. 'This lady would like to tell you about her problems', he said. The evangelist looked straight at the lady and asked: 'Woman, have you talked to God about these things?' She confessed she had not. 'Well go and talk to Him,' retorted the evangelist, 'and stop wasting the pastor's time!'

Why do people seek help from others? Often because of the inadequacy of their own relationship with God. They are content to use the better relationship of the one to whom they go, rather than devote themselves to prayer and the Word and to meet with God themselves. They want to use someone else as a crutch rather than develop their own spiritual relationship with God.

Often they are spiritually lazy people. Even when told what to do by someone who counsels them, they don't do it and still return for further help.

This is not to say that we should never seek counsel or advice from other believers. Far from it. We all benefit at times from the encouragement others can give us and the wisdom they can speak into our lives, but never as a substitute for faith in God and in His Word. The Lord says:

Counsel and sound judgment are mine; I have understanding and power (Prov. 8:14).

When people come to you for help they often expect you to pray over them for a quick solution to their problem. They want the power of God to come upon them to resolve all the things that concern them. Often it is revelation of the Word they need before prayer, truth before power. **Your prayer may alleviate the problem for a short time; but unless they are walking in the truth they will very quickly fall back into bondage when the next difficulty arises.**

Some will think that in coming to you they will receive their answer through your faith. God expects believers to believe! It is fine for them to believe together, to agree in faith; but not to look to others as a substitute for faith in Jesus.

THE AUTHORITY OF THE WORD

It is important to establish that the one you are seeking to help acknowledges the authority of God's Word. Without that submission to the Word, there is not a proper submission to God Himself, for He cannot be separated from the Word He has spoken.

Neither will there be the faith that can come only from learning to trust God over and above negative thoughts, feelings and circumstances.

Those who love Jesus will not only respect His Word; they will obey it, which is another way of saying they will believe it and act upon it. And the Father and Son come to make their home with such a one!

Jesus replied, **'If anyone loves me, he will obey my teaching. My Father will love him, and we will come to him and make our home with him.** He who does not love me will not obey my teaching. These words you hear are not my own; they belong to the Father who sent me' (John 14:23–4).

One crumb from the table was enough to heal the woman's child. God's Word sets before us the whole feast. Jesus is the Word of God; He is the living Bread that has come down from heaven.

I am the bread of life. He who comes to me will never go hungry, and he who believes in me will never be thirsty (John 6:35).

Again the emphasis is on coming directly to Jesus; on believing personally in Him.

You come **with** the one you are seeking to help, not **for** him.
You believe **with** him, not instead of him!
In Proverbs we read:

> My son, pay attention to what I say; listen closely to my
> words. Do not let them out of your sight, keep them within
> your heart; for they are life to those who find them and
> health to a man's whole body. Above all else, guard your
> heart, for it is the wellspring of life. Put away perversity
> from your mouth, keep corrupt talk far from your lips. Let
> your eyes look straight ahead, fix your gaze directly before
> you. Make level paths for your feet and take only ways that
> are firm. Do not swerve to the right or the left; keep your
> foot from evil (Prov. 4:20–7).

We must note a number of key truths from this passage:

1 **A 'son' is being addressed** – someone in a personal
   relationship with God.
2 **This son is to pay close attention to the words God speaks
   to him.**
3 **He is not to let them out of his sight!**
4 **They are to be kept in his heart.** He has to receive them into
   his heart by believing them before he can keep them there.
5 **These words are life to him,** not simply good advice.
6 **They will bring health to his whole body.** God works from
   the inside outwards. Satan attacks from outside and tries
   to get into the believer's thinking. If the life of God's
   Word is in his heart, then health will radiate from the
   believer's spirit through his soul and will even give life to
   his mortal body.
7 **The 'son' is to guard his heart** so that nothing that
   contradicts God's Word is allowed to take root there.
8 **His heart is a 'wellspring' or fountain of life if filled with the
   truth of God's Word.** From that source life will well up
   within him.

9 **He is to put away perversity from his mouth.** He is not to say anything about himself, others or his circumstances which contradicts what God says. Any such contradiction is perversity. A Christian can say the right things in the prayer meeting, when being counselled or when on his guard. It is what he says at other times that reveals what is truly in his heart.

10 **He is to keep corrupt talk far from his lips.** If he believes the truth, he will speak the truth and live by the truth.

11 **'Your eyes are to look straight ahead',** the child of God is told – not back, not in at himself, but straight ahead.

12 **He is to fix his gaze directly before him.** This means he is not even to **glance** behind him!

13 **He is to make level paths for his feet.** He does this by walking in the truth. John said:

> Dear friend, I pray that you may enjoy good health and that all may go well with you, even as your soul is getting along well. It gave me great joy to have some brothers come and tell about your faithfulness to the truth and **how you continue to walk in the truth** (3 John 2–3).

Why was Gaius's soul getting on so well and why was he enjoying good health? Because he was faithful to the truth. He continued to walk in the truth.

14 **The believer is to take only ways that are firm,** rocklike. The only way to do this is not only to hear the Word, but put it into practice!

15 **He is not to swerve to the right or left.** He is not to turn from the truth of God's Word by listening to men's ideas or opinions. Neither is he to allow himself to be drawn into types of ministry which contradict God's Word.

16 **He is to keep his foot from evil!** If he continues in the Word, to abide in Jesus, he will walk in faith, in righteousness, living in the Spirit! This will keep him from evil!

> I say then: Walk in the Spirit, and you shall not fulfil
> the lust of the flesh (Gal. 5:16 NKJ).

You will notice by now that **we are not isolating healing from
the living out of the whole Gospel.** Neither are we coming to the
scriptures with some interpretation that will support precon-
ceived ideas. We are seeking to see what the Bible teaches us
about who a Christian truly is and how he is to live as a result.

SPEAK THE TRUTH

**We want the Word itself to shape our thinking, inform our
speech and be the basis for our actions.** Those who only listen to
God's Word but don't do it are deceived:

> **Do not merely listen to the word, and so deceive yourselves.
> Do what it says** . . . But the man who looks intently into the
> perfect law that gives freedom, and continues to do this, not
> forgetting what he has heard, but doing it – he will be
> blessed in what he does (Jas. 1:22,25).

James also emphasises the importance of what the Christian
says. The tongue can bring either blessing or curse. It is like the
rudder of a ship. Although only a small part of the body it
directs the course of the person's life.

We would all like to think that God directs the course of our
lives. He certainly wants to. In reality we can sin and be
disobedient, rebellious, or simply unbelieving, in which case
we steer off-course from the way God intends. Repentance will
bring us back on course; but it is better not to go off-course in
the first place!

If the heart is a fountain of life because it is filled with the
truth, then the mouth will speak the Truth. **Many curse
themselves by speaking negatively about themselves, instead
of blessing themselves by speaking the Truth** – the words that
are Spirit and life. How important, then, to agree with God's

perspective on your life and to tackle negative issues in the way His Word indicates.

Set a guard over my mouth, O Lord; keep watch over the door of my lips (Ps. 141:3).

You place your life under the words you speak. We all experience conflicting thoughts within and have to question whether they are of God, self or even the enemy! We have to choose which of these conflicting thoughts to believe. What we say is the proof of the choice we have made!

Refuse, therefore, to say anything about yourself or others that conflicts with God's revelation of truth.

David understood the importance of God's Word:

Preserve my life according to your word (Ps. 119:25). Strengthen me according to your word (v. 28).

I run in the path of your commands, for you have set my heart free (v. 32).

Your word is a lamp to my feet and a light for my path (v. 105).

For your love is ever before me and I walk continually in your truth (Ps. 26:3).

For the word of the Lord is right and true (Ps. 33:4).

The law of the Lord is perfect, reviving the soul (Ps. 19:7).

Dare we substitute anything else for the Truth? To love people is to love them with the Truth, even if this involves confrontation. At all times we are to speak the Truth in love. We are not to allow our love or the use of our time to be manipulated by those who do not want the Truth!

God has given us the Counsellor to guide us into all the Truth, not to help us avoid its claims upon us. Freedom comes through believing that truth, not denying it!

12   Counselling the Seriously Hurt

For some the process of conversion can only be accomplished over a period of time. It is truly a matter of rescuing them from the dominion of darkness, of lifting them out of a deep pit.

To explain what this involves I am going to take an extreme case. Perhaps you will never have to deal with such a situation, but if you see what is involved in this act of rescue, you can apply the necessary principles to other cases. For obvious reasons I have used a different name for the person concerned.

Sally was born into a satanist family and dedicated to Satan at birth. She was brought up to hate, not love; to curse, not to bless. She was abused as a child and placed in prostitution as a teenager to lure men into satanism. She was taught that her body belonged to the devil and had to be given to him. So she commonly experienced 'orgasm' with demonic powers.

Sally became pregnant and gave birth, only for the child to be taken from her immediately for ritual sacrifice. Although throughout her pregnancy she knew this would happen, it was a traumatic event for, having given birth, she found to her surprise that she wanted to keep her child.

She grew more and more desperate but could see no way of escape from her situation. She came to us through others who had been delivered from satanism. She knew nothing of the Gospel, except the distortion of it taught her by satanists.

Sally had great fear of the blood of Jesus that would be the very means of her deliverance. (Satanists are taught that if they take the cup at Holy Communion they will die immediately.)

The first thing was to accept Sally and give her the opportunity to get out of her situation by offering her a home while she was led out of darkness into light. She moved into one of our households with those who would be directly responsible for ministering to her. Another girl shared a room with her for reasons which will become clear.

During her time there Sally was abducted by satanists while out for a short walk near the place where she was staying. She was subjected to horrific sexual torture, but finally released because she had been 'de-programmed' as her abductors put it.

What they meant was that by that time she had been born again and so refused to renounce Jesus, despite the torture. She had learnt how to resist the enemy, instead of yielding to his demands.

After her return she was attended by a Christian doctor and loved back to full health by her household.

Now, many years later, completely set free from her past by Jesus, Sally is working with needy children and is a faithful witness for her Lord and Saviour. How was she brought out of such terrible bondage? By the Truth, brought to her by the love and power of the Holy Spirit working through believers.

It was not a question of taking Sally back into her past; who would want to revisit a past like that? But during the process of coming to Christ she needed to pour out to Him the black and evil things stored up within her. This could only happen over a period of time.

On each occasion those helping her encouraged her to bring all these vile things to Jesus and gave her assurance of His forgiveness. At first this was not easy for her to receive, but the speaking out of the evil within her brought a certain release. Slowly she was able to believe that Jesus not only forgave her, but accepted her and was ready to give her a new life, make her a new person. For this she began to long.

In the early stages the nights were often extremely difficult. Not only was she subjected to nightmares but also to visitations of the demonic powers to which she had given her body for sexual 'intercourse'. The young woman sharing her room would stand with her in prayer, teaching her to resist the enemy.

It was not long before Sally was able to commit her life to Jesus Christ. She had certainly been through deep and thorough repentance. She was then baptised in the Holy Spirit so that she could herself exercise authority over the enemy and all his forces.

She was now taught, not only the power of the blood and the cross, but her place and inheritance in Christ. Her grasp of the Truth was to be crucial during the time of her abduction.

As a believer she now needed to be fruitful for the Lord. Within a few months of coming to us, she was a radiant Spirit-filled believer, part of our ministry team and able to minister to others.

She travelled with me on occasions and sometimes gave a very powerful testimony at evangelistic meetings. **She would emphasise that her situation and deliverance were due to the power of the cross. Her understanding of who she was now in Christ had completely transformed her life and enabled her to know that God could use her.** The past no longer existed; the Truth had set her free!

In the early stages of her Christian walk the enemy would make renewed attacks on her encouraging her to look back. He tried to produce physical symptoms to suggest that she was not truly set free. Sally learnt to resist all these attacks.

Many were deeply affected by her testimony and turned to Christ. However, before one meeting when she was due to give her testimony again, the Lord made it clear to me that she should not do so. He had been pleased to use her in this way for a season, but knew the cost to her in having to review such a past. (Sally was always discreet about what she said publicly.)

When I told Sally what the Lord had said to me she replied:
'I'm so glad you said that. I never used to have any problems
giving my testimony, but on the last couple of occasions I have
found it difficult. I felt the Lord saying that He didn't want me
to look back any more – not even in testimony.'

Sally did testify again, but not about her past – only about
what God was doing in her in the present.

As the Holy Spirit took charge of Sally's life, He chased out
all the areas of darkness. There was no need to do any digging
or delving!

THE NECESSARY INGREDIENT

If it is possible for someone like Sally to be set free, become a
vibrant believer and a fruitful child of God's Kingdom, loving
and ministering to others, then this must also be possible for
others whose history and problems seem insignificant by
comparison.

Many believers have been brought up in Christian homes,
belong to churches, and still are not free. They are forever
looking back or within, living more in defeat than victory.

And yet others come out of backgrounds where there has
been drug, alcoholic and sexual abuse, who have encounters
with the Lord, believe what He did for them on the cross, are
set free and never look back. They immediately become
witnesses to others with similar backgrounds. Many are in
full-time ministry within a few months of being saved, full of
evangelistic zeal and fervour.

Why should there be such discrepancy? Not because God
favours some more than others. **The truth of what He has done
on the cross is the same for all. The inheritance every believer is
given in Christ is the same. Each has the same Word in his or her
Bible and the same Holy Spirit living within.**

So what is the difference? In a word, FAITH. Some have
their backgrounds where they need to be: behind them! Others
are always looking back, forever looking in and analysing

themselves – and are even encouraged to do so by their 'counsellors'.

The truth is that each born-again believer, no matter what his past, is crucified with Christ; he has died. It is no longer he who lives but Christ who lives in him. The only way for him to live now is by faith in the Son of God who loves him and gave His life for him, that he might be set free completely.

It is for freedom that Christ has set us free. Stand firm, then, and do not let yourselves be burdened again by a yoke of slavery (Gal. 5:1).

Paul affirms that the Gospel, 'is the power of God for the salvation of *everyone* who believes' (Rom. 1:16). This is true for everyone – irrespective of how awful, traumatic or damaging their past life has been.

The Gospel is not the power of salvation for everyone who is counselled, but for everyone who believes! Hence the need to bring people, even seriously damaged people, into faith in the Truth. Without that faith, even those with minor problems will wallow around in introspective failure and defeat.

Those who counsel need, therefore, the dynamic of faith in their own lives. They also need to have a firm grasp of the Truth. They cannot convey to others what they do not have themselves! It is easier to try and apply some system of ministry than to walk in faith and obedience to God's Word. There has always been the temptation to prefer law, even 'counselling' law, to faith.

COMPLETE SALVATION

Because Jesus has met every need on the cross:

He is able to save completely those who come to God through him, because he always lives to intercede for them. Such a high priest meets our need (Heb. 7:25,26).

What Jesus has done on the cross is complete. He was able to cry out in triumph just before His death: 'It is accomplished' or 'It is finished'. Everything needed for our total salvation has been completed.

Jesus saves *completely* all those who come to God through Him. And He always intercedes for them! He stands before God on your behalf!

The amazing prophecy in Isaiah, chapter 53, gives a vivid description of the meaning of the cross. Not only did Jesus carry our sins, He also met every human need in that act. **He was identified with us, that we might be totally identified with Him.**

His appearance was so disfigured beyond that of any man. (Isa. 52:14).

Even the disfigured can identify with Jesus because He was identified with them.

He had no beauty or majesty to attract us to him, nothing in his appearance that we should desire him (Isa. 53:2).

Those who have no natural beauty, or who do not think of themselves as beautiful, were on that cross with Jesus.

He was despised and rejected by men (v. 3).

All who feel despised and rejected can know that their condition was shared and overcome by Jesus. He suffered rejection to deliver us from rejection and make *any* who put their trust in Him totally acceptable in God's sight.

He took up our infirmities (v. 4).

All sickness was overcome by Christ's victory at Calvary.

And carried our sorrows (v. 4).

He met every need of body and soul on the cross.

Yet we considered him stricken by God, smitten by him, and afflicted (v. 4).

All the afflicted find their Saviour in Jesus; in what He has already done. Those who think God has given them a rough deal in life can know that Jesus was given the roughest deal of all in order to set them free from every need.

He was pierced for our transgressions, he was crushed for our iniquities (v. 5).

He took all sin upon Himself; He was even crushed so that all who feel burdened, crushed even, by their sins, their failure and need, could be set free.

The punishment that brought us peace was upon him (v. 5).

Because He has punished Jesus for your sins, God will not punish you for them as well. God will not punish the same offence twice. The price has already been paid for you to have peace with God, no matter how grave your sins.

And by his wounds we are healed (v. 5).

The healing of every person's need in spirit, soul or body, took place on the cross. God does not have to do anything further to give us that healing. Faith in Him and what He *has done* releases God's healing power into our lives.

When you confess your sins, Jesus does not have to be crucified all over again so that you can be forgiven. He has done the work already. You are laying hold of the forgiveness made possible through His finished atoning work.

The same is true for your healing. Jesus does not have to do anything more than He has already done. Faith lays hold of

His finished healing work. The shedding of His blood makes it possible for us to be whole in spirit, soul and body.

You can see already how Sally needed every one of these truths about the crucifixion to become real in her experience. It was not a question of trying to heal her soul life, but of leading her to Jesus, to the cross, so that she could be delivered completely from the past. She had to be taught the Truth that she needed to lose her soul to Jesus in order to find it. And as she submitted her soul to God so the power of His Holy Spirit began to infuse her soul life to create the character of Jesus in her.

The former condition of the believer does not alter the fact that every Christian has to lose his soul. He has to be prepared to reckon himself dead or he will struggle to live the new life, and will experience more defeat than victory.

The Gospel works! The Truth really does set people free! Even a former satanist can become a beautiful, Spirit-filled child of God, radiating the love and person of Jesus – through faith in what He has already accomplished.

The Lord has laid on him the iniquity of us all (v. 6).

Yes, even the worst of those iniquities have been laid on Jesus. All the sins of unbelief, all the negativity that grips so many people. All was laid on Him!

He was oppressed and afflicted (v. 7).

Jesus was oppressed to the extent that He cried out: 'My God, my God, why have you forsaken me?' (Matt. 27:46). But through His victory on the cross He overcame all the oppressive powers of darkness, so that any who have been bound by Satan can be set free.

And having disarmed the powers and authorities, he made a public spectacle of them, triumphing over them by the cross (Col. 2:15).

To God the old life of every believer is as unacceptable as Sally's. It is not a matter of degree. The flesh is the flesh and cannot be improved, accepted by God or healed.

Once again we can see the truth of what Jesus taught us: 'Repent and believe the good news.' There is a simplicity in the Gospel which causes it to be powerful and effective to *anyone* who believes, of any race or culture, and of any intellectual ability.

It is often those who exalt their reason above the Word, their souls above the Spirit, that find it difficult to accept humbly the work of the cross in their lives. As Paul has pointed out:

> We preach Christ crucified: a stumbling-block to Jews and foolishness to Gentiles, but to those whom God has called, both Jews and Greeks, Christ the power of God and the wisdom of God (1 Cor. 1:23–4).

No wonder he went on to say:

> I resolved to know nothing while I was with you except Jesus Christ and him crucified (1 Cor. 2:2).

Jesus shared the lot of the broken-hearted and was Himself wounded so that:

> He heals the broken-hearted and binds up their wounds (Ps. 147:3).

Isaiah chapter 53 begins with a question:

> **Who has believed our message and to whom has the arm of the Lord been revealed?** (v. 1).

And there is the heart of the issue! 'Who has believed?' We do not need sophisticated ministry techniques; we only need to

believe what He has done! **To all those who do believe, the arm
of the Lord is revealed! They experience the power of God's
Word, of His truth setting them free.**

For the message of the cross is foolishness to those who are
perishing, **but to us who are being saved it is the power of God**
(1 Cor. 1:18).

Through what happened to His 'physical body through death',
Sally is made holy in God's sight, without blemish and free
from accusation (Col. 1:22).

You who once were far away have been brought near
through the blood of Christ (Eph. 2:13).

She came to realise that her every need had been met on the
cross. No wonder Jesus cried: **'It is done!' 'It is accomplished!'
'It is finished!'**

13 Confronting with the Truth

If someone seeking help needs to be brought to genuine repentance, then the only effective way to help him is to bring him to repentance.

If he is not in a position of faith about the matters which overcome him, you need to teach him the truth, praying as you do so that the Holy Spirit will cause the Word to become revelation to His heart.

If he is being disobedient, is self-centred or self-obsessed, instead of denying himself, taking up his cross and following Jesus, then you will need to confront him with Jesus's claims on his life. The truth is often confrontational, as Jesus demonstrated in His ministry.

If the one who seeks help is living in resentment and bitterness because he has not forgiven those who have hurt or rejected him, then you need to show him his need to forgive.

OBEDIENCE

Can you hear what is being said? **In all these situations it is not healing that is needed, but obedience to God's Word.** Obedience will bring about significant changes in a person's circumstances because that obedience will be the product of significant changes of attitude.

It is not true to say of any born-again believer that he or she cannot obey God's Word. It is to enable precisely this that God Himself in the person of the Holy Spirit has come to live in him or her!

Therefore everyone who hears these words of mine **and puts them into practice** is like a wise man who built his house on the rock. The rain came down, the streams rose, and the winds blew and beat against that house; yet it did not fall, because it had its foundation on the rock. But everyone who hears these words of mine and does not put them into practice is like a foolish man who built his house on sand. The rain came down, the streams rose, and the winds blew and beat against that house, and it fell with a great crash (Matt. 7:24–27).

The difference between the man who built on rock and the one who built on sand is that the former put the Word into practice while the latter did not! **Notice, both heard the Word; but while one did it, the other didn't!**

If you have someone before you who is not putting the Word into practice his life will remain on sand until he does so. It is your responsibility, therefore, not to comfort him with a few moments of prayer, but to face him with his need to live the Truth – not just listen to it! This is the route to freedom which is why Jesus said:

If you hold to my teaching, you are really my disciples. Then you will know the truth, and the truth will set you free (John 8:31–32).

He also makes it clear that anyone who loves Him will obey His teaching (John 14:23). So disobedience to God's Word is a demonstration that a crisis of love towards Him exists on the part of this particular person. Anyone who loves, concentrates on the one he loves. Nothing hinders denying self and loving

Jesus more than a wrong love of self, a love of the flesh rather than the things of the Spirit.

Those who are guilty of this self-love will not usually thank you for making them aware of it, and may even deny this is true of them. In fact, they may claim to hate themselves, not love themselves, because they have such a low estimation of themselves.

To love self has nothing to do with how you view yourself but on how much time you spend thinking about yourself, being concerned about self, speaking about yourself, concentrating on yourself and all your problems!

A mother may have a delinquent child who causes her great concern. Yet, for all his faults, this child is her child and she loves him – no matter what he does to test that love, or to cause her to be exasperated with him.

In much the same way many Christians live in constant disappointment with themselves, but this does not make them any the less self-centred or self-concerned. They continue to love the self-life, even though they are fed-up and frustrated with themselves.

There is no point in ministering into a self-life that is to be denied, or to heal a life that is to be reckoned dead.

DEAD TO SIN

We must appreciate that some suffer unnecessary defeat, however, because they do not believe they have died to sin. Their sense of failure stems from the fact that it seems sin is very much alive in their lives. They expect to sin, so they do!

The flesh cannot be disciplined; it has to be denied altogether. **To indulge the self-life in just one area gives the whole of that self-life power over you.** Instead of recognising the need to reckon yourself dead to sin and alive to God in Christ Jesus (Rom. 6:11), one area of disobedience keeps that self-life very much alive and influential!

To battle against the flesh is self-defeating, as we have seen, and results in confusion. While protesting that he hates his flesh life, many a Christian does the very thing that maintains its influence over him; he talks about it! He only does this because he does not truly believe he is crucified with Christ or that the scripture is right when it tells him that he died to sin.

When we do not proceed according to God's Word He allows us to suffer defeat, until we are prepared to put into practice what He says. At that point the Word becomes rock beneath your feet.

Many are concerned about the works of the flesh, but not the flesh itself. They refuse to die! They know they belong to Christ Jesus but refuse to believe what this involves.

Those who belong to Christ Jesus have crucified the sinful nature with its passions and desires (Gal. 5:24).

This verse does not say that the believer needs to crucify his flesh; it states that because he belongs to Jesus he *has* crucified his flesh together with these desires he knows to be contrary to God's will.

Many suffer defeat because on the one hand they want victory in a particular area, but refuse to deny themselves to obtain the victory. A person may hate himself for having lustful desires and yet still read pornographic magazines or watch X-rated films! A person with a problem of greed may talk about wanting to diet while tucking into another cream doughnut.

The flesh is in direct opposition to the Spirit. It is only by denying self and walking in the Spirit that a person becomes self-disciplined. This 'self' is not allowed to run his life.

Regeneration does not alter the flesh; it gives you a new life, makes you a new creation so that you no longer need to live according to the flesh, but are now empowered to live the new life. The flesh, with its desire to sin, is overcome by concentrating on the new life by fixing your attention on Jesus, not constantly looking at yourself.

The self wants to lead; so does the Holy Spirit. Who is to be given the pre-eminence?

THOSE WHO WANT TO BE HELPED

Remember, it is deception to hear what God says and not to do it. **You cannot minister to deception. You can only expose it so that the person can repent of it.**

> The man who says, 'I know him', but does not do what he commands is a liar, and the truth is not in him (1 John 2:4).

Sometimes you may wonder whether a particular person really wants to be a disciple and follow Christ, whether he has any intention of living by the Truth, or even if he wants to be healed. This may seem harsh, but it is better not to waste time on those who are unprepared to submit to Jesus. You cannot help them until they are prepared to acknowledge His authority in their lives. It is better to devote your time to those who genuinely are looking to Jesus to help them; those who are prepared not only to look at the medicine bottle but to take the spiritual medicine it contains, even if the Truth seems unpalatable at the time. One thing is certain: it will do them good!

The enemy is good at sending his emissaries, those who will take your time, sap your energy, but who have no real desire to serve Christ. These are usually the demanding ones!

In the early years of my ministry the Lord showed me how to distinguish between those He led to me for help, and those who were the enemy's deploys. The former would show deference to how busy I was; there would be a humility and graciousness about their attitude. The others would be demanding and manipulative. They were not concerned with Christ's way, but only in getting their own way!

> This is the verdict: Light has come into the world, but men loved darkness instead of light because their deeds were evil

. . . **But whoever lives by the truth comes into the light,** so that it may be seen plainly that what he has done has been done through God (John 3:19,21).

Why have former generations, which have experienced such remarkable revivals and general outpourings of God's Spirit, not needed soul-healing as it is practised today? Because the cross was preached and people were 'soundly converted'. They were not asked to raise a hand or come forward to make some token act of commitment. They were truly born again because the preaching confronted them with what was expected of them as believers: a holy and righteous lifestyle. They had to face the issue of sin at the very outset. **They were not led to a counsellor but to Christ,** and were taught that their whole trust and confidence must be in Him alone.

They 'prayed through' to a saving knowledge of Jesus, often with tears and sometimes over a prolonged period, not just a few minutes.

Many want a solution to a particular crisis, but without cost to themselves. They would prefer to continue to live self-indulgent, carnal, disobedient lives, using the excuse that they feel unable to believe or to pray. Instead of overcoming the flesh they are overcome by the flesh, and do not want to take the necessary steps to alter this situation.

Even some who have received the Holy Spirit are soulish; they are not prepared to deny themselves in order to follow Christ. They are so full of self-concern that they will talk about themselves at every opportunity. **They want attention, not self-denial. They want to survive, not die!**

Those who want to love and care for such people will not help them by pandering to their wishes. Jesus would never compromise His claims on people's lives. On one occasion 'many of his disciples turned back and no longer followed him' (John 6:66) because they found His teaching too demanding. On another occasion a rich young man went away sorrowful because Jesus told him that his wealth prevented him from following Him.

Jesus is not a spiritual pill to be taken for a headache; He is the Lord of glory who is drawing to Himself a people for His glory. **It is not His purpose for people to take hold of Him to bolster up or 'heal' the self-life which is to be denied, reckoned dead, crucified with Him and buried in the waters of baptism!**

SOULISH LIVES

Some years ago I asked the Lord why the move of the Holy Spirit that the churches were enjoying, usually called the charismatic movement, was having so little effect on the world. You would think that if God was enduing His people with power from on high, there would be a considerable impact on the nation, as there has been in times of genuine revival.

The Lord made clear to me that although He had made available all the resources of His Spirit to His children, most were still living soulish lives. They were trying to use His resources for their own soulish ends instead of for their intended purpose. So the evangelistic zeal of the early years of the charismatic movement, when great numbers of people came to a saving knowledge of Jesus Christ and were filled with the Holy Spirit, had been followed by years of inward-looking longing for soul-healing on the part of many.

Did the enemy hijack what began as a genuine move of God? You can come to your own conclusion. The Church is to fulfil the great commission to make *disciples* of all nations. Jesus's call to disciples is to deny self (not concentrate on self), take up their crosses and follow Him – out into the world, not into an endless series of healing seminars!

We experience healing as we respond to God's call with obedience and faith, not by becoming introspectively soulish. It is the devil's lie to say: 'I can't follow Jesus until all these wounds of the past are dealt with.' They have already been dealt with!

Jesus's call to the disciples to follow Him came at the beginning of His relationship with them. 'My sheep hear my voice and follow me', He said. This means He is walking ahead of you and you are following behind. If you turn around and go back into the past, you have turned your back on Jesus. That is walking away from Him, not following Him. Instead of reckoning the old dead, buried and finished with, you are proclaiming by your actions that you believe it is very much alive and has an influence over you greater than Jesus Himself!

When praying with someone who thought himself unusable by God because of his considerable personality problems, the Lord gave me a simple question: 'What do you do with a delicate, out-of-shape, china tea-pot? Answer: Make tea in it, of course!' God does not wait until we attain a state of perfection before He uses us. If that were the case He would have no one to use.

The secret of receiving from God is not to concentrate on self, but to look away from self. It is in giving that you will receive. Paul says:

I pray that you may be active in sharing your faith, so that you will have a full understanding of every good thing we have in Christ (Philem. 6).

It goes without saying that the Christian needs to know the Truth so that he has a faith to share. The more he speaks this out to others the more he is built up in that faith himself, and able to live in the good of the truth he is proclaiming.

PAST PROBLEMS

The more a person concentrates on his problems, speaking about them, the more he is stuck with them. He needs to speak of these things only once as he brings them to the cross of Jesus. He can then be sure that what he has spoken of is 'under the blood'.

It goes without saying too that there are things in our lives which should not be suppressed or buried; they need to be brought out into the open, into the light of Jesus so that they are then dealt with by the power of the cross.

There have been many occasions when I have had to listen lovingly and patiently while a person 'unburdens' himself. Then, together, we can bring these matters to Jesus – SO THAT THEY WILL NEVER BE SPOKEN OF AGAIN.

If, subsequently, the person tries to go over the same ground again, I will immediately stop him. 'Stop! That has already been brought to the cross. It is already dealt with.' 'I don't *feel* that it has gone', may be the reply. In which case I will point out: 'You will never *feel* that it is dealt with until you *believe* what Jesus has done for you. **The right feelings will follow faith, not precede faith!**'

With such people you have to be loving but firm. It does not help them if you allow them to manipulate you into spending time going over the same ground again and again. To do so is to give ground to the enemy and feeds the false idea that some deep work of deliverance is needed. This has led to great bondage for some who have been subjected to hours of so-called 'deliverance' which it seems is never completed; there always seems to be something more, something deeper, something farther back. The person is left wondering how he will ever get to the root cause of it all, how long it will take. He is helped momentarily, or so he thinks, because of the prayer and attention he has received; but he is no nearer believing the Truth: THAT HE IS DEAD AND HIS LIFE IS NOW HIDDEN WITH CHRIST IN GOD.

He is no nearer reckoning himself as dead. Quite the opposite. He has lost ground because he fears he will never be completely free to live the new life, as there are still nasties from the old life holding him back. We can see how readily deception has come into this whole process.

Can a born-again believer have problems that relate to his past? Most definitely. But the way to deal with these is not to go back into the past. He has a problem as to how to relate to his past. This simple diagram will help explain this:

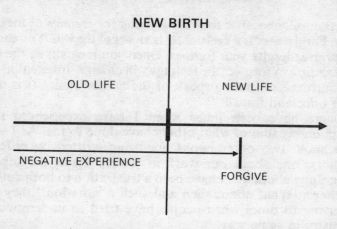

The cross separates him from his old life. He does not have to go back into the 'flesh' in order to live in the Spirit. Such a suggestion is spiritually ridiculous. **You would not suggest that a person has to relive sin in order to be forgiven. The fact that he confesses it to Jesus and brings it to the cross is sufficient for the miracle of forgiveness to take place.**

And once under the blood it is never to be mentioned again. It is dealt with once and for all. So with any other need from the past.

FORGIVE AND FORGET

Why should this person talk again and again about certain things from the past? Because he has not forgiven those who perpetrated those things. Therefore the bitterness, resentment and hurt remain.

It is no small thing to forgive those who have caused rejection, rape, abuse and other traumatic events. However this is Jesus's method of 'inner healing'; and the only one which truly works! As soon as the person is willing to forgive those that have caused the hurts, the 'healing' follows.

Some will claim they cannot forgive. This is a common

reaction only because they are looking for *feelings* of forgiveness. **Forgiveness is a decision; it is an act of the will. You choose to forgive, despite your feelings.** Once you have taken the step of deciding to forgive, the feelings will change. Inherent in this is your decision not to speak of the matter again! It is dealt with once and for all.

There have been times when I have experienced deep rejection because of what others have done to me. As I write this book, two other books are being written by different authors: one about our work at Roffey Place, the other a biography about me. I have been a frustration to both authors at times. 'What about such and such a situation?' they ask, referring to times when people have tried to undermine my ministry in some way.

'What about it?' is my reply.

'What have you to say about it?'

'Nothing!'

'Nothing? Why not?'

'Because I have forgiven the people concerned. Therefore I am not free to speak of those matters again. It is as if those things never happened!'

To their credit both authors have accepted this, although as writers no doubt regretting having to omit what to some would have been interesting reading!

Jesus says we have the authority to forgive or to retain sins. As He has shown us such great mercy, dare we refuse to be merciful to others? **How dare we hold on to hurts when Jesus will never hold against us the things He has forgiven!** They are forgotten; there will not be any mention of them again, even on the Day of Judgment. It is as if those sins had never happened.

And so it must be with the hurts we have received. **The one who refuses to forgive is a victim of his own lack of mercy.** The more a person appreciates how merciful God has been to him, the easier he will find it to be merciful to others. Those who are forgiven much, love much!

Of course every Christian needs to forgive immediately those who grieve, hurt, persecute or reject him, so that no root of bitterness grows up within him.

Anyone who is truly repentant has certainly tasted God's abundant mercy. An unrepentant Christian needs to repent before healing is ministered to him, and if necessary he needs to forgive any who have wronged him. Jesus said:

For if you forgive men when they sin against you, your heavenly Father will also forgive you. But if you do not forgive men their sins, your Father will not forgive your sins (Matt. 6:14–15).

'I can't forgive' is often a cover-up for 'I am unwilling to forgive'. The resentful person's attitude is: 'Why should I forgive? It was not my fault! I was the one who was wronged. Why should they be let off, they deserve to be punished. They don't know the misery they have caused me – and they don't care! Why should I forgive?'

Where emotions are involved reason is easily distorted. The spiritual answer is clear: **'You need to forgive. You will remain a victim, not of the hurts so much as of your own unwillingness to forgive, until you do!'**

I have found it helps others greatly when I explain that forgiveness is a decision. You choose to forgive. You do not wait until you have the right feelings before you make the right decisions.

To forgive, a person does not have to be taken back over past events to relive them, any more than he has to relive past sins! **His problem is not in the past, but how he relates to the past.**

Anyone can sit down and consciously remember past hurts if he is foolish enough to do so, just as he can remember past sins. I can remember the events in my life that have caused me great distress, but because I have forgiven those concerned I can think of these events with no pain. What is the point of speaking of these things? I am better employed in speaking the truth in love to encourage others and build them up in Christ!

What of the deeply hurt personality who has suffered such great traumas that the events have been blotted out from conscious memory? It is best to leave such cases to those qualified to deal with them. However, anyone ministering in the power of the Holy Spirit is able to use the gifts of the Spirit. It should never be necessary to go digging and delving into a person's past. The Holy Spirit is able to give words of knowledge and wisdom which will penetrate to the heart of the matter and show how to deal with it speedily.

When praying with people the Holy Spirit has frequently made me aware of something in a person's past. When I have questioned him or her the response is often: 'Oh, I'd forgotten about that' – not because the matter had been forgiven, but buried. There and then the person can forgive and be set free from something that has been allowed to influence them subconsciously for years, without ever realising that this was the case!

Realise now that you do not need to allow anything from your past to hinder you in living the new life.

And when counselling others beware of those who constantly make excuses for themselves because they are unwilling to face the cost of following Jesus. They do not want to deny self, but talk about self. They don't want to obey the Word, only excuse their disobedience. They are unwilling to devote themselves to prayer and the Word, to seek God and meet with Him. So they meet with you instead! Their claim of 'I can't' is really 'I won't', or even 'I stubbornly refuse to'. Instead of drawing near to God in His love, they try to manipulate love from you!

You will not help them by allowing them to do so. Lovingly, gently, but firmly lead them into the Truth that will set them free!

14 Some Counselling Principles

We have seen that the first thing to do is to ensure the person before you is a born-again believer and has been baptised in the Holy Spirit. Once this is established how are we to proceed?

It must be made clear that the one counselling needs to be led of the Holy Spirit. So there can be no set formula. Every person and situation is unique. To try and apply some ministry technique will only result in bringing people into bondage, not freedom.

There can be no substitute for anointing. Never try to minister like some other person does; that also is bondage. You are unique and the Holy Spirit wants to operate in and through you to help others. It is not a question of reading a book or going to a series of seminars to learn how to do it, trying to apply someone else's system.

I am not going to give you a system. I would not dare to use one myself. This chapter will contain a series of useful hints, of 'do's and don't's', learnt from thirty years' experience of seeing the truth set people free.

You do not have my anointing, and I don't have yours. If you believe God is calling you to help others, then receive from Him the anointing to go with the call. Do not assume that you have the anointing automatically. The call and the anointing are distinctive.

It is the anointing that breaks the yoke of bondage (Isa. 10:27 NKJ). The proof of the anointing is the way the Spirit moves upon others as you minister the Truth to them.

If God has called you to a particular ministry, He is certainly prepared to anoint you for that ministry! So don't model yourself on someone else's anointing; get your own!

So here are some principles of how to counsel others with the Truth, principles I believe you will find useful:

1   **At least half (if not more) of your attention needs to be on what the Holy Spirit is saying, rather than on what the person is saying.** The Holy Spirit will take you directly to the heart of the problem, if you listen to what He is saying. And that may be very different from the perspective the person has about his need.

Often you have no way of knowing whether the person is telling you the truth. He may want to conceal something because he fears your reaction or rejection. Very few people will tell someone they don't know, the deepest secrets of their hearts; they are even less likely to tell someone they know well, as they have to live in relationship with that person afterwards.

2   **Treat the information you receive from the person as potentially unreliable.** It may be the truth; it may not be. The person may be acting out a role they have been playing for years. So it may sound very plausible. This is not to suggest that everyone you help is insincere or deliberately setting out to mislead you. It is simply to warn you not to accept everything that is said to you at face value!

3   **Realise that many will say what they think they ought to say.** Everybody likes to be accepted by others. It will be important to the person that you accept him. So this desire is likely to affect what he reveals, even subconsciously. He may not want to hide anything, but dare not verbalise the very thing that needs to be said.

4   **There is the kind of personality that sets out to shock you deliberately.** His testimony is even more unreliable. He is likely to say a series of outrageous things which at best are gross exaggerations, at worst downright lies!

5   **The person has come with a specific intention in mind. You need to determine as quickly as possible what that intention is.** He wants you to minister into that particular area, not other areas. Most want a quick, slick answer to their dilemma. They do not want to be confronted with the inadequacy of their prayer life (which may be why they come to you, not Him), their ignorance of or disobedience to His Word. Yet these things almost certainly have a direct bearing on the situation, and its solution.

6   **The information you receive from the Holy Spirit is far more reliable.** How do you know that the Holy Spirit is leading you? At one level you cannot be sure; there is always an element of trust. Not every thought you receive is from the Holy Spirit! Experience helps. But your ability to hear God clearly comes from your own relationship with Him. I normally spend at least half an hour a day (often longer) listening to what God says to me. It is difficult to turn on His voice like a tap simply because you are in a counselling situation. The Lord wants each of us to be sensitive to His voice at all times.

7   **Use the gifts of the Spirit, even while the other person is speaking.** Ask for a word of knowledge to bring you directly to the heart of the problem; or a word of wisdom to enable you to know how to deal with it. In some situations you will need to use the gift of discerning of spirits.

8   **Learn to listen carefully to, and take heed of, the 'inner witness of the Spirit'.** The Holy Spirit shows us when a person is being sincere or false; He will give you the question to ask or the appropriate word to speak, even though you may not understand its particular relevance.

9   **When the Spirit reveals something to you follow it through sensitively.** You are not there to judge, accuse or condemn.

Suppose a believer comes with a particular business problem. Everything is going wrong, he is facing potential bankruptcy. He has prayed about the matter but has received no direct guidance from the Lord. So he comes to you for help.

While he is speaking, the Holy Spirit speaks the single word 'adultery' to you. What are you to do in such a situation?

You could stop him in his tracks and accuse him of adultery, but you need to test what you have heard.

I would ask the man: 'Are your relationships pleasing to God?' He may say they are. In which case I will continue to listen to the Spirit. If this 'witness' about adultery continues, I will put the question more directly: 'Have you ever had an adulterous relationship?' He may say that he has never had such a relationship, or only in the past before he was a believer.

If the witness of the Spirit is that he is lying then I need to be stronger still, but without direct accusation. I might say: 'As you are speaking I believe God is telling me that you are having an affair with another woman, and this is why you cannot get through to God as you pray about your financial situation.' You are submitting what you believe to be the truth about his circumstances.

At this point the man is likely to realise that he is discovered and confess to the sin, but not necessarily so! If he confesses then you need to use the Lord's resources of love, grace and mercy to restore the brother, making it very clear that the relationship needs to end. It is very likely that he has been in considerable conflict because of the situation and has needed someone to help him face the issues.

10   **If you see clearly the answer to a person's dilemma, help the person to see this answer for himself.** That is more effective than your telling him the answers.

11   **Do not be afraid to confront the person of his need to repent if that is appropriate; and encourage him to be specific about the issues about which he repents.** Remember that unbelief concerning the problem facing him is often a sin that needs to be faced.

12   **Your purpose is to build and encourage faith where it is**

lacking. Faith comes from hearing God's Word. So it is more important for the Holy Spirit to give you a Word that will encourage faith, than for you to give loads of spiritual advice.

13   **Jesus healed 'with a word'. One sentence from God will do more than many sermons.** So don't preach! You can tell the person the solution and find him completely unmoved. So . . .

14   **You will be amazed at the way people change simply by hearing the Truth. The Truth imparts life to people when they believe it.**

15   **If faith for a specific issue is lacking ask the Holy Spirit to speak a word of revelation to the person, either directly or through you.**

16   **If the matter needs more extensive teaching of the Word so that the Truth can set him free, arrange for a suitable time to do this.**

17   **Get to prayer as soon as possible with the expectation that God will speak into the person's heart either directly or through a word He gives you.**

I have learnt that you can correctly analyse the situation and tell the person the solution, all to little or no effect. But when God gives you a particular word of truth in prayer, the person immediately experiences release. He needs the truth of the Word in the power of the Holy Spirit.

18   **You may need to speak with authority against some work of the enemy.** However, in the case of a believer, you need to encourage him in this. A fuller treatment of this is given in Chapter 20.

19   **It may be appropriate to lay hands on the person, not as a friendly gesture, but to impart some particular blessing from God.** The time to do this, then, is when you and the person for whom you are praying expect God to do something specific!

It is good to ask the person what he expects to receive from God. If faith is already present in his heart, encourage him to be specific about what he is asking and expecting to receive. If he has only vague hope, open the Word to him before praying. Faith comes from hearing the Word.

20   **Because you want to encourage the believer in his walk with God, avoid the temptation to do the work for him.** Ensure that he is involved as fully as possible. Do not pray his prayer for him; encourage him to pray aloud, no matter how simple or halting his prayer. And do not be over-concerned that he does not include everything you would have said. It is the prayer of the heart that God answers. Maybe not everything needed is going to happen on this one occasion. The Lord is much more patient than most counsellors!

21   **So do not go beyond what the Holy Spirit is leading you to do on this particular occasion, just because you want to see more happen.**

These are, I repeat, a few helpful hints. They are not the twenty-one laws of counselling!

There is a great temptation to take short cuts, especially if time is pressing. If teaching is needed then arrange a suitable time with the person. Meanwhile it would be helpful to encourage him to read some faith-building book or booklet that is particularly appropriate to his need, especially suitable sections of the Bible!

THE RIGHT PASTORAL SETTING

When fulfilling my itinerant ministry I will refer a person in need of teaching to a local pastor, saying that this person needs to know his place in Christ, or to understand the cross or whatever aspect of the truth is relevant.

Sometimes the person is attending a church where the Truth of God's Word is neither taught nor believed. All sheep need to be fed – with the Truth! It is no wonder so many struggle if they are trying to survive on a diet that is based on tradition, men's views of life, or teaching that is experience based rather than being revelation of God's Word.

The Resource Centre of Kingdom Faith distributes teaching materials, books and tapes to many who seek to survive in such situations. These are faith-building materials, which will greatly encourage the person in his personal discipleship and walk of faith, but cannot be a substitute for belonging to a congregation of vibrant faith.

It is unfortunate that many languish in places where they do not receive the teaching they need because of an emotional or soul bondage to a denomination. They fail to realise that their true loyalty is to Jesus Christ. God is glorified by the fruit we bear. So every believer needs to be in a place where he will be raised up and released in ministry to be fruitful, rather than be stifled by the unbelief of the leadership!

Of course there are many fine denominational congregations where the truth is taught and practised and where people are released to be fruitful. It is also true that there are fellowships where the truth is taught, but there is little evidence of anointing and freedom in the Holy Spirit.

All this is encouragement to pray and believe for genuine revival in the Church, which will certainly involve a return to vibrant faith in God's Word and evidence of the life-giving power of the Holy Spirit at work among His people.

All too often the itinerant minister is expected to do in a few minutes what can only be done properly over a period of time in a pastoral setting.

15   The God of Promise

When teaching those already believers, Jesus made it clear that He expected them to believe. When we look at Jesus's teaching on prayer, we once again see the centrality of faith in what He said. Believers were encouraged to believe together in their prayer, meaning that when they were at one in their faith they could be sure of the answer they would receive from the Lord:

> Again, I tell you that if two of you on earth agree about anything you ask for, it will be done for you by my Father in heaven. For where two or three come together in my name, there am I with them (Matt. 18:19–20).

To be gathered in the name of Jesus is to be gathered together in faith! Jesus said:

> If you believe, you will receive whatever you ask for in prayer (Matt. 21:22).

'Whatever' must include healing or anything else for which we pray with faith. At first this seems a dangerous promise for Jesus to make. Does this commit our heavenly Father to give us what He does not really want us to have? Not at all, as other prayer promises make clear. He does say that we can have whatever we wish, but on certain conditions:

If you remain in me and my words remain in you, ask whatever you wish, and it will be given you (John 15:7).

To live in Jesus is to live in the good of the position He has given us by virtue of our new birth. If His words live in us, we will both believe and obey them. These two things belong together. **If you believe, you obey. And if you obey, it is because you believe!**

Many believe the scriptures to be the divinely inspired revelation of truth. Assenting to the fact that the Bible is the truth is not the same as putting your faith in that truth. **In practice the only parts of the scriptures that we truly believe are those that we obey.**

Jesus intends His words to live in those who live in Him. He knows well that when this is the case we will live in submission to Him; and because His words live in us, we will not ask for anything opposed to His purposes. We will not be able to pray with any real conviction or faith for anything that opposes His will, for the Holy Spirit will inspire faith only for those things which are in line with God's purpose. It is important to take note of this inner witness of the Holy Spirit.

The outcome of praying for 'whatever we wish' under these conditions is that the Father will be glorified:

This is to my Father's glory, that you bear much fruit, showing yourselves to be my disciples (John 15:8).

There is no doubt that Jesus links this fruitfulness with answered prayer:

You did not choose me, but I chose you and appointed you to go and bear fruit – fruit that will last. Then the Father will give you whatever you ask in my name. This is my command: Love each other (John 15:16–17).

Live in Jesus, let His words live in you; then you will be fruitful and the Father will give you whatever you ask in Jesus's name. This is the clear sequence of thought in what He teaches, and of the way in which this teaching is worked out in our lives. This reinforces the central message of this book: **living in the Truth will set us free, not only from our past, but also to live the new life – to live and pray with faith.**

In John 14:12–14 there is another sequence of thought:

I tell you the truth, anyone who has faith in me will do what I have been doing. He will do even greater things than these, because I am going to the Father.

And:

I will do whatever you ask in my name, so that the Son may bring glory to the Father. You may ask me for anything in my name, and I will do it.

Let us note these following points:

1   What Jesus says is preceded by the phrase, 'I tell you the truth . . .' signifying that He is saying emphatically that what follows is the truth, even if His hearers find it difficult to believe.
2   He is talking about *anyone* who has faith in Jesus.
3   **Anyone who has faith in Jesus will do what He has been doing:** listening to the words of His Father, being submissive to Him, proclaiming the presence of the Kingdom, acting with the authority of the Kingdom and demonstrating the works of power that accompany the Kingdom! This, He says, of *anyone* who believes!
4   The believer will do even greater things, for he will be able

to pray for the Holy Spirit to come upon people; something Jesus could not do during His humanity as the Spirit was not yet given because He was not yet glorified (John 7:39).

5   Jesus will do whatever you ask in His name as you live in faith and obedience.

6   In this way the Son will bring glory to the Father. God is glorified in you by the faith that leads to answered prayer.

7   You can ask for anything in Jesus's name and He will do it, because you are living in His Word.

It is all too obvious from these scriptures that many Christians look to others to pray for them with the hope that this will produce the necessary miracle, but without living in faith and obedience themselves. We must not be tempted into pandering to them in this way. The commission the Church has received is to make 'disciples' of all nations; and disciples seek to live by faith and in obedience to the Lord.

A WAY OF LIFE

Faith is a way of life: 'The righteous will live by faith' (Rom. 1:17). To live by faith is to live in Jesus and allow His words to live in you.

We dare not substitute anything else for what God says in His Word. **It will not be surprising to see poor results if we do not pay due attention to this need for faith and obedience in those we are seeking to help.**

This does not mean that we have to attain some state of advanced perfection before God answers our prayers. Quite the contrary. New believers see the Lord answering their prayers in ways that usually amaze them. But then they usually find no great difficulty in living in faith and obedience to the revelation of Jesus they have just received.

The God to whom we pray is the God of grace, and all that He does in us is the work of His grace. Every answered prayer is evidence of His grace. It is not that our faith and obedience earn us the right to answered prayer. **These, however, are the best, the most favourable, conditions for the grace of God to work effectively in our lives.**

It is amazing that God seems to give us so many answers when there is little faith or obedience. But it is clear that we should not presume on His grace. Paul asks:

> Shall we go on sinning, so that grace may increase? By no means! (Rom. 6:1).

Because faith is a way of life, abiding in Jesus and His words abiding in you, it is difficult to switch on faith because a particular need has arisen. This is why so many Christians turn to others for help. **Because they are not living by faith, they do not have faith for the particular situation facing them.**

Prevention is better than cure. Those who live by faith take the shield of faith against the enemy's attacks and with the sword of the Spirit, the Word of God, attack the things which oppose them.

Some have said to me: 'I don't belong to a faith church.' I feel like asking them: 'Do you belong to an unbelief church then?'

> Everything that does not come from faith is sin (Rom. 14:23).

> The only thing that counts is faith expressing itself through love (Gal. 5:6).

How important it is, then, not only to live a life of faith and obedience yourself, but to be part of a congregation committed to such a lifestyle of 'faith expressing itself through love'. Not faith in tradition, but in God's Word. Not just a friendly, loving group of people, but those who demonstrate their love for Jesus by their obedience to Him. 'If you love me, you will obey what I command' (John 14:15).

In His love and grace, God does not wait until we attain an advanced stage of spirituality before we see His power at work in our lives, or before answering our prayers.

Each believer needs to be obedient to the revelation of truth the Lord has given him. In helping people, therefore, we want to encourage their faith by speaking God's Word to them. We can assure them that they are able to put His Word into operation through the power of the Holy Spirit.

There is a great difference between counselling the disciple who loves the Lord and diligently seeks Him because he wants to glorify Him, and the one who is casual about prayer, the Word and his or her discipleship.

Those living in faith and obedience do sometimes need someone to stand with them in faith. With others it soon becomes apparent that they would be happy to lean on your relationship with God, instead of developing their own! This is why it is important to direct people to the Lord, to His Word which builds faith encouraging them to *live* in the good of what He has said and done.

It is no hardship to encourage those whose hearts are genuinely given to Jesus, no matter how immature they may be in faith. Such people are eager to learn and ready to apply the teaching of God's Word to their lives. Their attitudes are in stark contrast with those who hear, know well what they are to do, but don't do it! And yet it is the disobedient who are then prone to turn in judgment on God, blaming Him for the catastrophes which befall them.

It is tragic that so many who desire to glorify the Lord are in churches where they receive little teaching of the Word or encouragement in faith. Coming into a meeting elsewhere when faith is operating and God's Spirit is moving, they are quick to respond and often receive healing or the answer to some other need, only to return to their churches where nobody wants to know about the great things that have just occurred. They are too threatening for those bound by religion but not moving by faith – as was the case in Jesus's day!

GOD'S PROMISES FULFILLED

If we are learning to live by faith, we are learning to live by promise. Peter says that:

> Through these he has given us his very great and precious promises, so that through them you may participate in the divine nature (2 Pet. 1:4).

To live in Jesus, to live in God, to walk in the Spirit is, then, to live by these very great and precious promises. They are so great that frequently they seem beyond us; but this is only because God is so much greater than we are. Paul describes Him as the one:

> Who is able to do immeasurably more than all we ask or imagine, *according to his power that is at work within us* (Eph. 3:20).

This is the new life! Sharing in the divine nature, abiding in Jesus! His mighty power at work within us enabling us to live as children of His Kingdom.

Beware of divorcing the promises God gives from any conditions that He attaches to them. For no matter how many promises God has made, they are 'Yes' and 'Amen' in Christ (2 Cor. 1:20).

> Since we have these promises, dear friends, let us purify ourselves from everything that contaminates body and spirit, perfecting holiness out of reverence for God (2 Cor. 7:1).

We want to walk in the holiness of God, to seek first His Kingdom and righteousness, and so inherit Jesus's promise that everything else will be added to us. Be wise about praying with those who are laying claim to some promise, but without paying attention to the conditions that go with the promise.

The time to pray and agree together is when they are concerned to see the conditions, as well as the promises fulfilled in their lives.

HOLD FAST TO THE PROMISES

'The testing of our faith proves that it is genuine', says Peter (1 Pet. 1:7).

None of us likes to be tested, nor do we like to be kept waiting when we want something. Jesus teaches us to persevere in prayer, to be determined to receive the answer needed. It is easy to grow impatient, or to begin soul-searching to see if there is any fault that is preventing us from receiving the answer; or to begin concentrating on the problem instead of the truth.

Consider it pure joy, my brothers, whenever you face trials of many kinds, because you know that the testing of your faith develops perseverance. Perseverance must finish its work so that you may be mature and complete, not lacking anything (Jas. 1:2–4).

Abraham 'did not waver through unbelief regarding the promise of God' (Rom. 4:20). **He was 'fully persuaded that God had power to do what he had promised'** (v. 21). So when someone has received a promise from God he has to hold fast to that Word believing God is faithful in fulfilling His Word.

The faith that perseveres, despite contrary circumstances, is the faith that is proved genuine and praises God. The one who stands the test 'will receive the crown of life that God has promised to those who love him' (Jas. 1:12).

So the one with genuine faith will not try to use you as a prop or substitute for his own relationship with the Lord; although he will appreciate your love and support during his time of testing.

It is important not to get in God's way when He is taking a believer through a testing time, a trial of faith!

You are helping him to keep his trust in God, so that He will supply his need. Where he has learnt to hold fast to God's Word and to pray through to victory, he will enter into a new dimension of faith that will stand him in good stead when facing future difficulties.

If a promise is not being fulfilled immediately, God must have good reasons for withholding the blessing. He is perfect in His timing. It may be that He will show you that the believer needs to sort out some particular area in his life. Maybe it is obvious to you, but not to him, that he is not truly in faith; he does not believe he has received the answer. You can encourage obedience or faith as the occasion demands.

This is your aim: to encourage dependence on Jesus and His promises, not dependence on you or any other human counsellor.

16 Fear

Unbelief in God's promises leaves the Christian in bondage to fear.

Fear is a soulish reaction either to certain thoughts or words (often inspired by the enemy), or to circumstances. Negative thoughts cause feelings of fear which can easily overwhelm a person. It is common for Christians to seek ministry for their 'fears', even to believe they need to be delivered from a spirit of fear. This is not usually the true nature of the problem. The believer does not have a spirit of fear:

> God has not given us a spirit of fear, but of power and of love and of a sound mind (2 Tim. 1:7 NKJ).

Why does he live in fear then? Because he allows his soul to dominate his spirit, instead of living in submission to God. So the life of his spirit is not able to influence his soul in the way God intends. Within his spirit there is power, love and a sound mind; but these qualities will not be real in his soul unless the Spirit has the pre-eminence in his life.

God's answer to fear is not to have the cause of your fear analysed. He simply says: 'Fear not' – no less than 366 times in scripture! He gives us good reasons for not being afraid: He promises to be with us always. If Jesus is with me, and His Spirit within me, I will only fear if I allow my soul to dominate my spirit.

I used to be an extremely fearful person, and my natural reaction in certain situations is still to be afraid. That is the response of my soul to the circumstances in which I find myself. If I dwell on those fears I will be paralysed into inactivity. So I have learnt to allow the Spirit to fill my soul with the Truth. This means I speak the Truth of God's Word to myself. I deliberately fill my mind with the Truth, so that my emotions can be influenced by that Truth, for then the fear will begin to evaporate. I cannot fear and trust at the same time.

I will often have to make a definite decision to move forward, despite any residual feelings of fear; for faith in God involves taking positive action. It is not a question of waiting until all the feelings of fear have gone before I step out in obedience to face the situation. Often we have to choose to obey God despite feelings of fear.

It is common for people to be afraid when they are confronted with the purposes of God. It seems He chooses people who will feel inadequate to His call on their lives so that they will put all their trust in Him.

The Lord makes it clear that this fear is a soulish response to what He asks of them. He makes it clear that it is not who they are that matters. He is not asking them to obey Him in their own strength. What matters is who He is and that He is the one who will be present with them to provide for them and protect them as they step out in obedience to Him.

The Lord said to Abram:

Do not be afraid, Abram. I am your shield, your very great reward (Gen. 15:1).

When Moses feared to return to Egypt to confront Pharaoh and lead God's people out of captivity, He said 'I will be with you' (Exod. 3:12). He could go in the name of 'I am who I am'. The Lord gave him assurance after assurance, and of course Moses fulfilled his task.

When the angel of the Lord appeared to Gideon as he was threshing wheat in a winepress for fear of the Midianites, he was assured, 'The Lord is with you, mighty warrior' (Judg. 6:12). When Gideon showed his reluctance to accept his commission, the Lord said to him:

> **Peace! Do not be afraid.** You are not going to die (Judg. 6:23).

Jeremiah was reluctant to accept his calling to be a prophet to the nations; the Lord was very firm with him:

> But the Lord said to me, 'Do not say, "I am only a child." You must go to everyone I send you to and say whatever I command you. **Do not be afraid of them, for I am with you and will rescue you,**' declares the Lord (Jer. 1:7–8).

And when God called Ezekiel to prophesy to His disobedient people, He said: '**Do not be afraid of what they say or terrified by them,** though they are a rebellious house' (Ezek. 2:6).

It seems that the Lord views fear as being the product of having faith in yourself. The answer, then, is simple: **Put your faith in Him, in who He is and His presence with you.**

This would not be a popular answer to fear in some counselling circles today! Nevertheless it is the Truth!

The person who is readily overcome with fear is allowing his soul life, rather than his spirit, to predominate. He believes the negative thoughts and feelings rather than allowing the power, love and sound mind of his spirit to infuse his soul with those qualities.

The Lord knows that we will all experience testing times, but He has given us wonderful promises concerning the way He will carry us through those times:

Fear not, for I have redeemed you; I have summoned you by name, you are mine. When you pass through the waters, **I will be with you;** and when you pass through the rivers they will not sweep over you. When you walk through the fire, you will not be burned; the flames will not set you ablaze. **For I am the Lord, your God, the Holy One of Israel, your Saviour** (Isa. 43:1–3).

You belong to the Lord; He has called and chosen you to be His very own. Therefore He promises to care for you in every way and to provide for every need:

And my God will meet all your needs according to his glorious riches in Christ Jesus (Phil. 4:19).

No matter how difficult the circumstance, no one and nothing can take His presence or His Spirit away from you, or separate you from His love, the perfect love that casts out all fear.

For I am convinced that neither death nor life, neither angels nor demons, neither the present nor the future nor any powers, neither height nor depth, **nor anything else in all creation, will be able to separate us from the love of God that is in Christ Jesus our Lord** (Rom. 8:38–9).

In all these things, Paul says, **we are 'more than conquerors through him who loved us'** (v. 37).

In the light of these truths, it makes little sense to concentrate on your fears or try to analyse their cause. Once your heart and mind are fixed on the truth, you will once again walk by faith and not fear.

The Lord said to Joshua:

I will be with you; I will never leave you nor forsake you (Jos. 1:5).

These were the words of strength and comfort he needed at that moment, faced with the great task of leading God's people to take possession of the Promised Land. Miracles would be needed to see their enemies vanquished. So the Lord impressed on him the need to live in the Truth, and gave him encouraging promises:

Be strong and courageous, because you will lead these people to inherit the land I swore to their forefathers to give them. **Be strong and very courageous. Be careful to obey** all the law my servant Moses gave you; do not turn from it to the right or to the left, **that you may be successful wherever you go.** Do not let this Book of the Law depart from your mouth; meditate on it day and night, **so that you may be careful to do everything written in it. Then you will be prosperous and successful.** Have I not commanded you? **Be strong and courageous. Do not be terrified; do not be discouraged, for the Lord your God will be with you wherever you go** (Jos. 1:6–9).

Living in faith and obedience to God's Word were crucial to the prosperity and success He promised Joshua.

And so with us. **The Lord wants you and every one of His children to prosper and be successful. This will only be accomplished as they choose to walk in the truth** (3 John 3–4). So the Lord warns Joshua not to be discouraged by his circumstances; He knew His servant would face difficulty as well as triumphant times.

The Lord wants your soul to prosper. So walk in the Truth and do not allow your circumstances to dominate your thinking.

The Lord's continual command to 'Fear not' is not a facile answer that avoids the real need. He knows it is the only answer that will meet the need.

Whenever you become 'soul-centred' you will be prone to fear, striving, failure and disappointment. Whenever you look at yourself or imagine that it is you on your own that has to face the difficult situation, you will inevitably have feelings of fear. This does not signify that God has taken His Spirit away from you, or that you need soul-healing. It simply indicates that you need to submit your soul life to the Spirit once again so that His life can infuse your soul with power and love. Then you will once again be able to rejoice in the Lord.

> Though the mountains be shaken and the hills be removed, **yet my unfailing love for you will not be shaken nor my covenant of peace be removed,** says the Lord, who has compassion on you (Isa. 54:10).

17   Physical Healing

On the cross Jesus did all that was necessary for physical as well as spiritual and emotional healing. Some deny this aspect of the cross because not everyone for whom they pray is healed. It is dangerous to construct doctrine from experience, rather than from the evidence of God's Word! **When we believe what He says, then we experience what He promises!**

The forgiveness made possible through the cross has to be appropriated by faith, just as physical healing does. Some ask God to forgive them again and again because they lack that faith. Some ask for healing again and again for the same reason.

In Matthew, chapter 8, the writer gives us an account of the healing that attended Jesus's ministry, healing of physical sickness and deliverance from demonic powers.

He drove out the spirits with a word and healed all the sick (v. 16).

Matthew then explained why these things were happening:

This was to fulfil what was spoken through the prophet Isaiah: **'He took up our infirmities and carried our diseases'** (v. 17).

There is no question that the writer equated both deliverance and the healing of all sickness with the work of the cross. But why should he quote the prophecy concerning the cross at this early stage of Jesus's ministry, before the crucifixion had taken place?

While on earth Jesus ministered to that particular generation, and then only in one place at a time. **The cross made the total work of salvation available to everyone of every generation everywhere!** It was a 'cosmic' event with eternal consequences.

Usually those who fail to teach the healing power of the cross see little healing in their ministries. When we do not see God doing particular things, it is very tempting to attempt to justify our lack of faith! Jesus said:

> **If you believe,** you will receive **whatever** you ask for in prayer (Matt. 21:22).

'Whatever' must include healing!

GOD'S WILL TO HEAL

The saving work of Jesus is the healing work of Jesus. It is God's very nature to heal:

> I am the Lord, who heals you (Exod. 15:26).

It should not be necessary to have to explain God's willingness to heal, but there is so much confusion concerning this topic it is important to communicate what God's truth reveals to us.

There is no question as to whether Jesus wants to heal. The first who came to Him was a leper who said: 'Lord, if you are willing, you can make me clean' (Matt. 8:2). **Jesus simply removed the 'if' and said: I am willing. Be clean!** (v. 3). Immediately he was cured of his leprosy.

People talk about the 'sovereign will of God' as an excuse when people are not healed. Surely God has declared His sovereign will in Jesus? He has shown that every need is met in Him crucified. The Lord will never deny faith in what Jesus has already accomplished.

We must remember that God does not always have His way in our lives. Do you ever sin? Yes, you do! Does God ever want you to sin? Is it ever His will for you to sin? Of course not!

God wills all men to be saved and has provided the sacrifice for us that makes this possible. But are all men saved? No, only those who put their faith in the saving work of Jesus Christ.

God does not sit on His throne as a fickle Father deciding whether to forgive this one or not, or heal that one or not. He has provided the means for us to be forgiven, saved, healed, set free. **When by faith we take hold of the Truth of what He has done, we see the fulfilment of what He has promised.**

Part of the present-day confusion comes from the fact that often people try to minister God's healing at the wrong time. Even Jesus could not perform many miracles at Nazareth because of the unbelief of the people!

When they came seeking healing, He would ask questions of them to see whether they believed they would receive what they asked. **Faith, remember, is being sure and certain!**

Often people receive the laying-on of hands without any enquiry as to what they believe will happen as a result. Neither is opportunity given for any repentance that may be necessary so that nothing will hinder the receiving of what God wants to give! Is the sick person in a right attitude of forgiveness towards others? If not, God will not forgive that person. And if he is not forgiven, he is unlikely to be healed!

Those who administer healing in a pastoral context can deal with all these points *before* prayer; and they will obtain better results if they do! The laying-on of hands does not have to be a spontaneous thing at a public service. At such times some receive healing, but many don't! It is discouraging both to the sick person and to the rest of the congregation, to see the same people coming forward again and again, without anything apparently happening to them.

ANOINTING

Often anointing is administered in a way that is not true to the teaching of scripture. Notice what James says:

> Is any one of you sick? He should call the elders of the church to pray over him and anoint him with oil in the name of the Lord. And the prayer offered in faith will make the sick person well; the Lord will raise him up. If he has sinned, he will be forgiven. Therefore confess your sins to each other and pray for each other so that you may be healed. The prayer of a righteous man is powerful and effective (Jas. 5:14–16).

1 **The sick person should call for the elders to go to him.** It was not for the elders to take the initiative. The sick person needs to exercise faith!
2 **The elders should pray over him.** They are to pray with faith.
3 **They anoint him with oil.** Both the sick person and the elders can see this as the point at which they believe healing is given and received.
4 **It is the prayer of faith that effects the healing.**
5 **There should be open confession of sin by those present, with the assurance of forgiveness, 'so that you may be healed'.**
6 **The prayer of the righteous person** (made righteous through Jesus) **is powerful and effective.**

Again we would see much better results if we ministered anointing in the way God directs.

All this goes to show that wherever possible, due preparation can take place before prayer or anointing. Of course this is not appropriate in cases of extremity, with very young children (although the parents should prepare their hearts), the mentally handicapped or for minor irritants where spontaneous prayer is obviously called for!

PREPARATION

When ministering physical healing in a pastoral situation I have found that a few days of preparation for the sick person has been of immense value. I will share what I have found effective, but not as a blueprint for everyone to copy.

1 Most healing needs have been present for some time; so a few more days will not make any significant difference.
2 God is concerned about the whole person, not just the sickness. So this is an opportunity for God to meet afresh with the believer, spiritually as well as physically.
3 The person needs to consider if there is any sin which needs to be confessed, any area of disobedience or any relationship where forgiveness is called for.
4 Is the person in a position of faith? If not, time needs to be given to reveal the scriptures to show that it is God's purpose to heal. It should not be taken for granted that the person believes this. Everyone knows God *can* heal; the issue is whether the person believes God *will* heal him or her **when we pray.**
5 I give the person three or four scriptures of promise appropriate to his need and suggest he sits quietly three times a day and allows God to speak them to his heart. (I suggest he uses the method of prayer explained in my book, *Listen and Live*.) Faith comes from hearing the Word, so I suggest he reads the healing miracles in the Gospels. He is coming to Jesus, not me, for healing; so I suggest he asks the Holy Spirit to make these words revelation to his heart.
6 I then arrange a time when we will meet to pray. I actually fix a time for the healing! 'Now let's fix the time for your

healing.' This gives a focal point. **He needs to come, not expecting prayer, but to receive his healing.**

7   When he comes for this appointment I ensure *he* prays. He has the opportunity to open his heart to the Lord, to ask for forgiveness, to confess any lingering doubts and to state what he believes God is going to do about his need.

8   I then pray in whatever way the Holy Spirit leads, giving assurance of forgiveness first if necessary, praying for the anointing of the Holy Spirit to be upon us before I minister the healing.

9   I will pray 'in the Spirit and with the mind also', if necessary taking authority over the enemy.

This is not a form of ministry to be used legalistically. You can see the benefit of building people's expectation. There are always those who say that this is dangerous in case people are disappointed! **If we do not expect healing to happen when we minister, then what is the purpose of praying?**

I cannot say that I have always seen the total healing take place when ministering in this way; **but something always happens.** The person meets with God, the healing process is begun, perhaps faith is enlarged. Often, of course, the healing does happen there and then. In any case, we thank the Lord for what He has done, for we are told that we are to pray at all times with thanksgiving.

It is advisable to prepare the ground as well as possible. Did Jesus prepare people like this? Most of the healings recorded were in an 'itinerant' context rather than a pastoral one, when obviously such preparation is not possible. However, Jesus did ask penetrating questions, the answers to which showed that the person was able to receive the healing.

Most of my ministry is now itinerant and I must confess to a certain frustration at not being able to prepare people to receive, although at a public meeting I will always lead in a time of repentance and stress the importance of faith before ministering healing.

I do not take people through the above process of preparation if the Holy Spirit gives witness to pray immediately.

MINISTER WITH AUTHORITY

Jesus commanded His Church to heal the sick. We have His authority to do this in His name. Although faith is the central element in healing, especially on the part of the one who is sick, it is also necessary for those ministering to exercise authority in this area of ministry.

We have already seen that we are only able to exercise authority inasmuch as we are submitted to the Lord's authority. Because Jesus was completely submitted to His Father, He could exercise perfect authority over sickness and the demonic powers which plagued people's lives. He gives that authority to believers:

> I have given you authority to trample on snakes and scorpions and to overcome all the power of the enemy; nothing will harm you. However, do not rejoice that the spirits submit to you, but rejoice that your names are written in heaven (Luke 10:19–20).

The reason that believers have such authority is because their names 'are written in heaven'. **They belong to God's Kingdom which is far superior in power to the dominion of darkness.** The Holy Spirit living in the Christian is far greater than the power of darkness operating in the world.

We shall talk about deliverance later. Here we need to see this as part of the total ministry of healing to which God calls His Church.

God's Spirit is now upon the believing Church to enable God's children to continue Jesus's war against sickness. He said of Himself:

> The Spirit of the Lord is on me, because he has anointed me to preach good news to the poor. He has sent me to

proclaim freedom for the prisoners and recovery of sight for the blind, to release the oppressed, to proclaim the year of the Lord's favour (Luke 4:18–19).

He told the messengers sent by John the Baptist to report what they had seen:

The blind receive sight, the lame walk, those who have leprosy are cured, the deaf hear, the dead are raised, and the good news is preached to the poor (Luke 7:22).

We can rightly say that God wants all people to be saved; but He knows that not all will be saved. We can say that God wants all to be healed; but He knows that not all will be healed. We can even go as far as to say that ideally God would not want anyone to sin or be sick; and He tells us to pray:

Your kingdom come, your will be done on earth as it is in heaven (Matt. 6:10).

We do not expect to find either sin or sickness in heaven. So Jesus waged war on both while on earth. We are to do likewise.

It is clear that Jesus healed all who came to Him, but He did not take the initiative of going to people to heal all the sick in Israel. Healing the man by the pool of Bethesda (John 5:1–9) was the exception rather than the rule.

Our aim must surely be to exercise the faith and authority to heal all who come to Jesus with faith. It is significant that Jesus asked such questions as:

'Do you want to get well?' (John 5:6).

'Do you believe that I am able to do this?' (Matt. 9:28).

Just because someone came to Him, Jesus did not take it for granted that he either wanted healing or had the faith to be healed!

He also made it clear:

> I tell you the truth, the Son can do nothing by himself; he can do only what he sees his Father doing, because whatever the Father does the Son also does (John 5:19).

If this was true for Jesus, it must also be true for us.

> By myself I can do nothing . . . for I seek not to please myself but him who sent me (John 5:30).

I would love to see every sick person healed at every meeting at which I spoke! But like Jesus, I have to be completely dependent on God's leading; and so do you!

I have found that speaking words of command following words of knowledge to be a most powerful way of ministering healing in a public context. The one ministering is dependent on the Lord to make him aware of the particular needs to be met. When he commands the sickness to depart, speaking with authority, the healing happens there and then.

On such occasions people have frequently said that as soon as the word of authority was spoken, the power of God came upon them and they were healed. There have also been occasions when people have said to me that they were healed as soon as I mentioned their particular sickness; and yet I did not speak any such word. When the Spirit moves in this way some obviously hear directly from God and are immediately healed.

There is an interesting scripture which says that:

> The power of the Lord was present for him to heal the sick (Luke 5:17).

Even in His ministry there must have been particular moves of God when many people received their healing.

We have seen that we should not isolate healing from the

whole Gospel. The exercise of authority is greater than commanding sickness to leave, but does include this. Jesus rebuked fever and it left immediately (Luke 4:39).

In His teaching on prayer, Jesus makes it clear that every believer is to speak with faith to the mountains of need.

> I tell you the truth, if anyone says to this mountain, 'Go, throw yourself into the sea,' **and does not doubt in his heart but believes** that what he says will happen, it will be done for him. Therefore I tell you, whatever you ask for in prayer, **believe that you have received it, and it will be yours** (Mark 11:23–4).

It is important to note that **the believer is to speak to the need himself, as an outworking of his faith; he is not supposed to be dependent on someone else to address the mountain for him!** When he speaks to the need he is to believe in his heart and not doubt that what he has said will come to pass.

Jesus makes it clear that to pray with faith means that we believe we have already received the answer to our prayer. This is different from the statements Christians often interpret as faith: 'I really believe God is going to do it.' That is hope, not faith.

> **Hope says it will happen.**
> **Faith believes it has happened, even when there is no immediate evidence to substantiate that.**

Authority is an outworking both of the believer's submission to God and of his faith in His promises. Jesus says that it is not the amount of faith that matters but the quality of it:

> If you have faith as small as a mustard seed, you can say to this mulberry tree, 'Be uprooted and planted in the sea,' and it will obey you (Luke 17:6).

Such faith is expressed by speaking to the need with authority with the expectation that there will be the desired result; faith inspired by Jesus who is the 'Author and Perfecter of our faith'!

DEALING WITH UNBELIEF

What can be done when counselling someone who does not have such faith in his or her heart?

1 **There is nothing you can do to change a person's heart.** This is the work of God alone.
2 **Pray that the person will receive revelation from God.**
3 **Encourage him to be honest with God about his unbelief or doubts.** He hates hypocrisy but loves honesty. He will forgive the unbelief.
4 **Encourage him to ask God to speak a word of faith to his heart.** This may happen at that precise moment or later, but the expectation is that God will speak such a word to him.
5 **When he has received such a word and has come to a position of faith, that is the time to minister healing to him.**
6 **The Lord may prompt you to pray for him before he has such a word; in which case you need to listen carefully as to how to pray on that occasion.** It may not be the right time to pray for the healing itself.
7 **When ministering remember that you are handling someone who is precious to the Lord. Whatever you do or say is to be in His name and is to be done, not only with authority, but with all the love and grace at your command.**

All ministry must be exercised in love if it is truly in the name of Jesus.

At all costs avoid wild, accusing, or condemning statements. These are said only out of your own frustration if you do not see things happening in the way you wanted or expected. It is easy, but does not help the situation at all, to blame the person with whom you are praying by saying he doesn't have enough faith, or there is some sin in his life that is preventing him from receiving the healing. This may be true, but **it is your responsibility to hear from God and bring a word of faith, correction or encouragement.** God never accuses us or makes us feel condemned; and you are speaking in His name!

So before ministering pray that the love of Jesus as well as His truth and power, will flow through you. You are speaking and acting in His name.

PART 3

OVERCOMING THE ENEMY

18 Opposing the Enemy

When dealing with those who were not believers, Jesus delivered them from the demonic powers which bound them, and then told them to follow Him. There is no evidence of His praying in the same way with those who were already believers. **Every believer has the responsibility to resist the enemy in his own life.** He is to submit to God and resist the devil who will then flee from him.

It is important, therefore, that every believer knows the authority he has over the enemy and how to exercise that authority. He needs to understand the enemy that opposes him, his tactics, and the various ways in which he tries to undermine his faith.

Believers have the authority to prevent and permit whatever is prevented and permitted in heaven. Jesus said:

I tell you the truth, whatever you bind on earth will be bound in heaven, and whatever you loose on earth will be loosed in heaven (Matt. 18:18).

To bind is to prevent; to loose is to permit. The Greek is difficult to translate simply. Jesus is saying that whatever is prevented in heaven, we have the authority to prevent on earth. Whatever heaven permits we can permit.

'Whatever' does not apply exclusively to demonic activity as we have seen, but must certainly include this. It is clear from Paul's teaching that we have spiritual opposition in heavenly places and this can affect what happens to us on earth.

> For our struggle is not against flesh and blood, but against the rulers, against the authorities, against the powers of this dark world and against the spiritual forces of evil in the heavenly realms (Eph. 6:12).

In this struggle, Paul tells believers to 'put on the full armour of God'. He uses the illustration of the pieces of armour to illustrate the essential elements in the Christian's defence against the enemy's attacks, and his ability to overcome him. These are:

1 TRUTH
2 RIGHTEOUSNESS
3 THE GOSPEL OF PEACE
4 FAITH
5 SALVATION
6 THE SPIRIT AND THE WORD
7 PRAYER

The Christian does not need to fall into such bondage that he needs someone else to take authority over the enemy on his behalf. He has the power to overcome the enemy himself! Each 'soldier' is to wear the armour, use the shield of faith and attack with the sword of the Spirit!

1 TRUTH: The Truth sets the believer free. **If he walks in the Truth he will walk in freedom and will not fall into bondage.**
2 RIGHTEOUSNESS: **If he lives in the good of the righteousness he has in Christ, he will not fall into serious sin.** When he does sin, he can confess his sins and will be forgiven and cleansed from all unrighteousness.

3 THE GOSPEL OF PEACE: Because of his faith in the cross of Jesus Christ, the believer has peace with God. Nothing can destroy his relationship of peace if he resists the enemy's attacks. The good news is that **he is at one with God, living in Christ and the Kingdom of God is within him.** He therefore has authority over the enemy, who has been thrown out of that Kingdom.

4 FAITH: **His faith in the Lord and His Word enables the believer to resist everything the enemy throws at him. He knows the Truth and can therefore resist his lies.** He knows his place and inheritance in Christ, so he can resist the enemy's attempts to make him doubt his worthiness, acceptance and love through Jesus. **He has the faith not only to survive but to overcome.**

5 SALVATION: **He knows that he is saved** and that this gives him a privileged position in relation to God, and power over the evil one. No one can snatch him away from Jesus.

6 THE SPIRIT AND THE WORD: The believer is filled with the Holy Spirit. **The One in him is greater than he that is in the world.** That Spirit of Truth guides him into all the Truth. So he can use the Word of God to refute the enemy, as Jesus did in the wilderness.

7 PRAYER: He is to pray in the Spirit on all occasions. **Not only will the Holy Spirit guide him as to what to pray, He will also fill his prayer with power.**

So God has made all these resources available to enable the believer to overcome the evil one. To walk in the Spirit is to walk in the Truth, to walk in the light, to live in Christ and allow His Word to live in him; then he will have nothing to fear, for he will be walking on the Highway of Holiness:

No lion will be there, nor will any ferocious beast get up on it; they will not be found there. But only the redeemed will walk there (Isa. 35:9).

'The unclean will not journey on it; it will be for those who walk in that Way' (v. 8). This is the place where only the Lord's children can walk.

The lion represents Satan who 'prowls around like a roaring lion looking for someone to devour' (1 Pet. 5:8). And the wild beasts are the demons which serve Satan. Those who walk on the Highway of Holiness are out of their reach. They may snarl and make angry-sounding noises; but they cannot actually touch them.

Sin and disobedience makes the believer vulnerable to the enemy's attacks, which is a good incentive to walk in right-eousness; but we do not always do what is sensible and right. We are told to ask for wisdom if we need it. Disobedience may seem relatively unimportant to the guilty one, but it is proof of a lack of wisdom. Those who disobey do not stop to think of the ways in which they are yielding themselves to the enemy's influence, making themselves vulnerable to him.

Persistent disobedience can certainly lead a person into bondage, even if he is a born-again Christian. Most of those bondages are broken by sincere heart repentance. **The power of the cross breaks the power of the sin that has temporarily bound the believer.** He only became bound through his own fault, through persistent disobedience or unbelief. Repentance restores him to the place of unity and peace with God.

THE NEED FOR WISDOM

But the wisdom that comes from heaven is first of all pure; then peace-loving, considerate, submissive, full of mercy and good fruit, impartial and sincere (Jas. 3:17).

Notice the qualities of this wisdom:

1 **It is pure.** To live in wisdom is to walk in purity, not sin. The wise choices are the right choices!
2 **God's wisdom is 'peace-loving'.** The wise believer will not

make decisions that disrupt his peace with God. He will choose righteousness, for sin causes him to lose this sense of peace.

3   **The wise believer is considerate to others.** He knows that faith has to be revealed in love, that the measure he gives will be the measure he receives back, that he will reap what he sows.

4   **He is full of mercy towards others,** because God has forgiven him for so much. He desires to have a forgiving heart.

5   **Because in wisdom he chooses to walk in the Spirit he bears much fruit for the Father's glory.**

6   **The wise man holds to the Truth, for then he will be impartial, judging everything by God's Word.** 'From now on we regard no-one from a worldly point of view' (2 Cor. 5:16).

7   **He has a sincere heart,** is a person of integrity and can be trusted.

Many of those who seek counsel have departed from the way of wisdom; hence the tensions and anxieties they experience. **It is not for us to judge them, but to bring them back to wisdom.** As we have seen this will inevitably involve the need of repentance, which restores a person to a relationship of peace and unity with God.

However, his lack of wisdom over a prolonged period of time may have led to real bondage in his life. It may seem to him that he cannot break free, that he needs deliverance.

BONDAGE

It is important for us to keep things in true perspective. Some want to blame demons for everything that goes wrong, so much so that they absolve themselves from blame. They refuse to face their responsibility for their sins or their need to repent.

There can be no doubt that the enemy opposes every

believer and uses demonic powers to accuse and deceive them. Many are oppressed because they have believed a series of lies which have come from the father of lies. Instead of exercising their authority to resist the devil, they have yielded areas of their lives to his influence.

Neither the devil himself, nor any of his demonic powers, have any rightful claims to a believer's life. The only ground they can occupy is that yielded to them by the believer – through sin, disobedience or by being deceived.

Nobody likes to face the fact that he has been deceived. We have all been deceived at times. We have all thought ourselves to be right when in fact we were wrong. That is the nature of deception!

God is infinitely patient with us. He does not judge or condemn us for being wrong or being deceived. **His Spirit gently but firmly leads us back to the Truth.** This may take time when we are full of self-righteousness, determined to defend a position we have taken because we do not want to admit we have been wrong. Because of pride we want to conceal from others that we have not only been deceived but have been used to deceive others. We have tried to influence them with our views which cannot be substantiated from the Truth!

Instead of holding on to pride, believers need to humble themselves before the Truth.

Although the Holy Spirit convicts the believer of sin, he is able to ignore this conviction if he so chooses. He can carry on with life, can still praise God and be aware of His love, yet resist the promptings of the Holy Spirit.

He may decide to persist in the sin. If he does so, it will take a greater and greater hold on him. At times he may feel uneasy about this because of the Holy Spirit's witness within him. But his love of the sin outweighs his desire to obey God; and so he persists in this area of disobedience. He thinks he can handle the situation; after all, God still loves him!

In time he will realise that this sin not only has a grip on him, but is affecting the whole of his spiritual life, his relationship with God and with others. He may pray about the matter, but for so long he has been deceiving himself, justifying the matter in his own eyes and even before God, that he cannot pray with much conviction or faith. The sin persists. He may seek someone's help, but without necessarily admitting to the real need. Or he may blunder on, putting on a good Christian front for others, while at the same time knowing he has slipped to a wretched state within himself.

His prayer life deteriorates, he loses his appetite for God's Word, which convicts him so clearly that he is loath to read it. He becomes tense and is prone to snap at those around him, especially those who love him. He grows withdrawn and morose.

He may come to the conclusion that if someone prayed with him he could receive a swift act of deliverance that would set everything right. A quick prayer of deliverance will do little good unless there is first genuine repentance. **He needs to submit himself afresh to God; then he can resist the devil himself with authority.**

The one who comes for prayer, but without true heart participation, may find temporary relief; but it is not long before the problem returns. This is because he has not faced the real problem: the condition of his heart.

He will need to repent of:

a the original area of sin and disobedience,
b persisting in this sin, ignoring the convicting work of the Holy Spirit,
c allowing the enemy to deceive him in this area of his life,
d instead of resisting the enemy, giving him ground on which to stand to accuse him,
e the way this sin has affected his relationships and attitudes to others.

His real sin has been to disobey the Lord. Like David he needs to admit: **'Against you, you only, have I sinned'** (Ps. 51:4). And so David's prayer is also pertinent for him: **'Create in me a clean heart, O God, and renew a steadfast spirit within me'** (Ps. 51:10).

Genuine repentance comes from the heart and must involve a definite turning away from the sin as well as a fresh submission of his heart to God. Then he will be able to resist the enemy once again. Nobody else can resist the devil for him, but others can stand *with him* against the enemy.

He may travel around seeking ministry from anyone he considers more able to exercise authority over the enemy. He will try the 'experts' in deliverance. But unless he is prepared for a change of heart, any help he receives will be short-lived in its effect, no matter who prays for him. The return of the bondage is likely to give him the impression that he is in a hopeless condition; that the enemy has a grip on him that cannot be shaken off.

His persistent disobedience has given demonic powers the opportunity to influence him and even exercise some hold over him. Those demons will have to respond to the prayer of authority from others who minister to this Christian. Hence the temporary relief. But without a change of heart the believer is likely to return to the sin and disobedience and so give ground back to the enemy.

Genuine repentance on his part, coupled with fresh submission to God and a determination to resist the enemy, is the only way for the problem to be dealt with effectively. He will not be able to sustain victory in any other way.

DEMONS

Christians should not be surprised that they are resisted by demonic forces. Whether they like it or not they are involved in spiritual warfare. **To refuse to fight is to give the field to the enemy.** Every believer needs to know, not only how to withstand these enemy forces, but how to overcome them.

Often Christians do not recognise when there is enemy

activity. They need to exercise the gift of the Spirit known as the discerning of spirits, and to pay attention to the inner witness of the Holy Spirit. He causes them to feel wrong about certain people and situations the enemy is using, even though it may not be apparent what exactly is wrong.

Satan uses demonic forces to oppose believers, even those who are seeking to walk in faith and obedience. He will try to deceive, to lie and accuse, in an attempt to draw the believer off course. The one whose heart is set on righteousness is not easily swayed or deceived; but the enemy will use every device he has to try and disrupt the believer's walk with God.

Lack of discernment by Christians when under demonic attack plays into the enemy's hands. Some even assert that demons are not real; that Jesus only talked of them because He was using the thought forms of the day!

That is a blasphemous suggestion for it accuses Jesus of deliberately deceiving people, which is the devil's work, not His. He brought people the Truth, often correcting their misconceived ideas. He would not have cast out demons from people if they did not exist! Neither would He have taught about them if He knew them to be a figment of people's imagination. He tells us some interesting facts about demons:

When an evil spirit comes out of a man, it goes through arid places seeking rest and does not find it. Then it says, 'I will return to the house I left'. When it arrives, it finds the house swept clean and put in order. Then it goes and takes seven other spirits more wicked than itself, and they go in and live there. And the final condition of that man is worse than the first (Luke 11:24–6).

1 Evil spirits or demons have personality. They are not vague powers or forces.
2 Demons can exist either within people or externally.
3 They seek places of rest. They want to take up residence within people if they can.

4   They can speak.
5   Demons can co-operate with one another.
6   They are able to plan and make decisions, so they have a certain amount of autonomy.
7   A 'clean house' is an invitation for greater demonic attack.
8   Some demons are more wicked than others.
9   They will take up residence wherever they are allowed to.

There is no doubt from either scripture or experience that the enemy attacks the soul of every believer. He even attacked Jesus at the level of the soul (and body when He was crucified), but could not have any influence over His Spirit. Because He lived in constant obedience and submission to His Father, He could exercise total authority over Satan himself, thus denying him any victory.

A disciple who walks in the Spirit, and so in the Truth of God's Word, will be able to exercise authority over every attack the enemy hurls against him.

Satan cannot steal your inheritance from you, but he will try to prevent you from living in the good of that inheritance. He can do nothing to change the Truth; so he will try to deceive you so that you do not live by the Truth. Then you will not be able to enjoy the freedom God intends for you.

Satan cannot take away the gift of eternal life you have received from God. Neither can he remove you from God's Kingdom. But he tries to steal the revelation of the Kingdom power and authority the believer has, because then he will not exercise his authority over the demonic forces deployed against him.

When the seventy-two returned to Jesus, delighted that even the demons submitted to them, He pointed out that this should not be their cause of joy. They needed to rejoice, not in the fact that they could overcome those powers, but why they were able to do so; their names were written in heaven. **They belonged to the Kingdom of light which is infinitely more powerful than the dominion of darkness!** Whenever light shines, darkness disappears.

They belonged to the Truth which is the answer to the lying, deceiving tactics of the evil one.

Because your name is written in heaven you have authority over every demonic force that opposes you. And you can exercise authority over the demons that attack others. Nothing will harm you, Jesus assures you. So you never need to fear those over whom you have power and authority.

This shows how irresponsible it is for Christians to allow themselves to get into bondage, either through sin or because they do not oppose those who come against them. To every believer is given the shield of faith in one hand, faith that enables him to resist everything the enemy throws against him. In the other hand he has the Sword of the Spirit, the Word of God.

Man does not live on bread alone, but on every word that comes from the mouth of God (Matt. 4:4).

With the Word of Truth he is able to overcome the lying, deceiving spirits which falsely accuse him. He needs to know the Truth that sets him free, and to live in the Truth which will enable him to maintain that freedom.

19 Deception

1 SELF-DECEPTION

Sometimes Christians want to be deceived. When a believer wants to hold on to some sinful area of his life and does not want to repent, the sin takes a firmer grip on him thus giving the enemy opportunity to place him in bondage.

We have also seen that the scriptures clearly teach us that **we are self-deceived when we hear what God says in His Word but fail to put it into practice:**

Do not merely listen to the word, and so deceive yourselves. Do what it says. Anyone who listens to the word but does not do what it says is like a man who looks at his face in a mirror and, after looking at himself, goes away and immediately forgets what he looks like. But the man who looks intently into the perfect law that gives freedom, and continues to do this, not forgetting what he has heard, but doing it – he will be blessed in what he does (Jas. 1:22–5).

These are the alternatives facing each Christian: to deceive himself through disobedience to God's Word, or to be blessed by his obedience.

It is clear that self-deception was already a problem in the early Church of New Testament times and took a number of different forms:

a   A person is self-deceived if he claims to be sinless:

If we claim to be without sin, we deceive ourselves and the truth is not in us (1 John 1:8).

b   A person is also self-deceived if he has exalted ideas about himself:

If anyone thinks he is something when he is nothing, he deceives himself (Gal. 6:3).

c   He is deceived if he thinks he can fool God:

Do not be deceived: God cannot be mocked. A man reaps what he sows (Gal. 6:7).

He will either sow to please his flesh, which is spiritual death; or he will sow to please the Spirit, which is eternal life. When Christians are perplexed as to why they should suffer certain problems, they need to consider what they have been sowing. A critical person reaps criticism. A judgmental person will be judged. Jesus makes it clear that he will be judged with the same judgment with which he judges others.

On the other hand, if he gives love he will reap love. If he is generous he will reap generosity and will not be in any need.

d   A Christian is deceived whenever he raises his reason and understanding above the revelation of God's Word:

Do not deceive yourselves. If any one of you thinks he is wise by the standards of this age, he should become a 'fool' so that he may become wise (1 Cor. 3:18).

All these expressions of self-deception are examples of the Christian elevating his soul or self-life above the Spirit. This always spells trouble.

e A man is also self-deceived if he appears to be a spiritual person, but speaks negatively, is critical and judgmental of others:

If anyone considers himself religious and yet does not keep a tight rein on his tongue, he deceives himself and his religion is worthless (Jas 1:26).

That seems a harsh evaluation of his religion. But Jesus said: 'For out of the overflow of the heart the mouth speaks' (Matt. 12:34). Jesus recognises that an unbridled tongue is a manifestation of a wrong heart.

f It is self-deception to imagine that formal religion is able to save people.

The difficulty with self-deception is that the guilty one usually fails to see his own sin. That is the nature of self-deception; it causes him to be spiritually blind. Try telling a critical person that he is critical and see the reaction you receive!

The Pharisees were the epitome of self-deception, performing their external religious duties while neglecting the most important elements of the law. Deceived because they imagined their words were pleasing to God, while their hearts were far from Him. Appearing righteous, yet full of corruption within.

Jesus warned against legalistic, formal religion. Paul also warned that the unrighteous would not inherit God's Kingdom:

Do you not know that the wicked will not inherit the kingdom of God? Do not be deceived: Neither the sexually immoral nor idolaters nor adulterers nor male prostitutes nor homosexual offenders nor thieves nor the greedy nor

drunkards nor slanderers nor swindlers will inherit the
kingdom of God (1 Cor. 6:9–10).

No universal salvation here! It is not a question of 'everyone
will be all right in the end'.

g **Imagining that everyone will go to heaven is another form of
self-deception.**

Jesus answered, 'I am the way and the truth and the life. No-
one comes to the Father except through me' (John 14:6).

h **A Christian deceives himself if he imagines he cannot be
influenced by others, by flirting with sin or temptation.**
Paul warns believers about the company they keep:

Do not be misled: 'Bad company corrupts good character'
(1 Cor. 15:33).

He has the responsibility to witness to all and sundry, but that
is not the same as allowing himself to be yoked with those who
will try to suck him into the standards of the world, who will
appeal to his flesh life and tempt him to compromise his walk
with God.

2 DECEPTION

Satan is out to deceive believers. Here are some of the
warnings we are given in scripture:

a **False Christs.** Paul says:

For if someone comes to you and preaches a Jesus other
than the Jesus we preached, or if you receive a different
spirit from the one you received, or a different gospel from
the one you accepted, you put up with it easily enough (2
Cor. 11:4).

There are many other Jesuses being preached today, even within churches. Some preach a Jesus who is powerless to intervene in natural circumstances, or to answer prayer supernaturally. Some preach a Jesus who is not the same today as He was yesterday. They claim that He does not heal today or perform the signs and wonders experienced in the life of the apostolic Church. They preach a partial Gospel, a partial cross, a partial Jesus even!

The Jesus in whom we are to believe is the Jesus of scripture, the One who 'is the same yesterday and today and for ever' (Heb. 13:8).

b   **False prophets.** Jesus warns believers:

> False Christs and false prophets will appear and perform great signs and miracles to deceive even the elect – if that were possible (Matt. 24:24).

All prophecy is to be tested, no matter who speaks or what miracles he performs.

c   **False teachers.** The enemy seeks to deceive through those who teach a distortion of the truth.

> Even from your own number men will arise and distort the truth in order to draw away disciples after them (Acts 20:30).

d   **False claims.** Jesus warns:

> Watch out that no one deceives you. For many will come in my name, claiming, 'I am the Christ', and will deceive many (Matt. 24:4–5).

e   **False teaching.** Not only will false teachers arise, but the enemy will attack Christians directly. Paul tells Timothy:

> The Spirit clearly says that in later times some will abandon

the faith and follow deceiving spirits and things taught by demons (1 Tim. 4:1).

These things that are taught will appear reasonable, and even spiritual, but are deceptive works of the enemy, such as new age teaching, spiritism and the occult. The Holy Spirit gives true discernment as to what is of God. If even the elect can be deceived, it is obvious that not all are prepared to listen to the inner witness of God's Spirit.

We are to believe the whole counsel of God, not be selective in choosing only what we want to believe and rejecting the rest. A lack of submission to the authority of God's Word opens the door to the devil's deceptions.

If you do not believe what God says you believe something else instead. You have substituted something else for the truth!

How important it is, then, not to give the enemy a foothold, ground on which he can stand to accuse, deceive or condemn. How important to walk in the Spirit, in the Truth and to test every spirit to see that it is of God (1 John 4:1).

Many obviously do not do this. It is amazing how often prophecies are apparently received by a congregation without being weighed or tested in the way scripture instructs us.

HOW CHRISTIANS CAN BE DECEIVED

Believers need to have a good grasp of the Truth of God's Word, or else they are an easy target for the enemy's deceiving tactics. Peter warns:

Your enemy the devil prowls around like a roaring lion looking for someone to devour (1 Pet. 5:8).

So he instructs:

Resist him, standing firm in the faith (v. 9).

Self-deceit encourages the enemy in his deceit. Jeremiah warns that: 'The heart is deceitful above all things and beyond cure' (Jer. 17:9).

For this reason at new birth God gives believers a new heart and puts a new spirit within them. But that heart can get dirty with use. Paul encourages us to:

> Purify ourselves from everything that contaminates body and spirit, perfecting holiness out of reverence for God (2 Cor. 7:1).

An unclean heart can easily be deceived. The serpent set out to deceive Eve in the Garden of Eden, and at that time her heart was right towards God. How much easier for his work to be accomplished if the heart is not right.

The way he set about deceiving the woman was by challenging the Word God had given to Adam. 'Did God really say . . .?' This is still his attitude; to challenge the believer's faith in God's Word, to cause him to doubt the authority of that Word, to set up his own ideas and reason against the Word. **Those he persuades to disbelieve will disobey the Word!**

Jesus says that those who are double-minded need to purify their hearts. Either you submit your mind to the thinking of scripture or you will inevitably be double-minded.

You also aid the enemy in his deceptive work if you push scriptural truth beyond what is revealed. The enemy often wants to push people too far so that they become unbalanced.

For example, the New Testament teaches clearly that we have authority to cast out demons. But it is clear by now that this is not always the answer to a person's problems. The one who sees a demon behind every problem, and deliverance as the answer to every need, will put many people into bondage instead of setting them free!

It is deceptive to engage in ministry which takes a person back into the flesh in order that he might be free to walk in the Spirit.

Again this is a contradiction to the truth of the Gospel, the good news of what Jesus Christ has done for us.

Believers are not to be like,

> infants tossed back and forth by the waves, and blown here and there by every wind of teaching and by the cunning and craftiness of men in their deceitful scheming. Instead, speaking the truth in love, we will in all things grow up into him who is the Head, that is, Christ (Eph. 4:14–15).

It is alarming to see how easily many Christians are misled by the latest fad of ministry, or how readily they will adopt one emphasis of scripture to the almost total exclusion of other emphases.

We are to speak the truth to one another in love, building up each other in God's Word. The more we do that the less likelihood there is of being deceived.

THE COUNTERFEIT

Satan's deceptions are embodied in false religions and cults which abound today. Some acknowledge Jesus, but not as God's Son. Others are completely ignorant of Him. Others still are directly and deliberately opposed to Him.

When a person turns to Christ it is important that he renounces completely his previous involvement in any of these activities. Jesus made it clear:

> He who is not with me is against me, and he who does not gather with me, scatters (Luke 11:23).

You cannot worship God and demons (1 Cor. 10:21). All counterfeit religions are demonic, worshipping false gods as if they were the truth.

Those who have been part of deceptive religions or cults need to be sure that their thinking has not been influenced by the

errors they previously believed. Once again we see how important it is for every believer to have a firm grasp of God's Word, which will bring correction to his thinking.

There is no place for superstition, fetishes or charms in a Christian's life. All such things must be destroyed along with any dependence there has been on them.

When ministering to people who have had occult connections or involvement with such organisations as Freemasonry, it is important that they themselves renounce these things. You cannot do this for them. If they renounce them, you can join in prayer that they will experience no residual influence on their lives from such things.

Likewise they need to renounce their involvement with eastern techniques of meditation, prayer or yoga. Also they need to stand against the negative spiritual effect of receiving treatment through certain alternative medical techniques which have occult roots. Some of these appear to do good physically, while placing the person in spiritual bondage.

Some have also been involved in 'therapy' which has been soul-centred and has therefore contributed to their longing and desire for soul-healing, instead of 'losing' their souls.

If an area of bondage persists despite prayer, a renunciation of former activities may well be needed, but must be coupled with an appropriation of the truth.

At first some may be reluctant to acknowledge the demonic origin of a religion or cult in which they have been involved. As we have seen, no one likes to admit he has been deceived. However, **walking in the Truth has to involve a renunciation of everything that opposes the Truth, whether in the past or present.**

Satan can appear as an angel of light. Sometimes there is a longing to hold on to 'culture'. There seems nothing wrong with this in itself; except that many cultures are intimately linked with the religions of those cultures. This is what leads to syncretism, the blending of different beliefs.

It was for this that God's people in Old Testament times

found themselves in persistent sin. They were frequently warned by the Lord not to intermarry with those of other religions, nor to have anything to do with their idols or religious practices. Their worship of the God and Father of Jesus Christ was to be pure and undefiled. When they failed to obey the Lord in this respect, trouble always resulted.

God is a jealous God (Exod. 20:5). He has chosen a people for Himself. Our faith cannot be in Him and in anyone or anything else at the same time. He expects a wholehearted obedience.

So-called 'inter-faith' services are another deception. It is claimed that this is a 'loving' thing to do and shows that as Christians we accept other people, quite apart from what they believe. But those of other religions are praying to what is false, and therefore demonically inspired. The truth and the false cannot be put together in that way.

The only way to love those who are deceived is to seek ways to share with them the Truth of Jesus Christ, not give them the impression that we respect their false gods and will join them when they pray to them.

Such attitudes are often called intolerant. It is right to be intolerant of what is false and deceptive. If we truly love people we want to see them delivered from their deception so that they embrace the truth. **It is better to be charged with intolerance than to be disobedient to the Lord.** To stand against deception is the way to love those who are deceived!

For some it is costly to renounce their former religion. It can lead to being isolated from families and even their nation; and perhaps losing their jobs as well. But to those who find life in Jesus Christ, the changes in their lives are so significant that the advantages far outweigh the cost, no matter how great.

There can be no compromising of the Truth, for whatever reason, in a Christian's life. Just as the Truth sets him free, so compromising that Truth will put him into bondage for this weakens his faith in Jesus.

PRAYER AND FAITH DECLARATION

Renounce areas of self-deception, asking the Holy Spirit to reveal things to which you have been blind. Encourage others to do likewise. When praying with them it is important that they renounce these things themselves rather than leave you to do this for them. When leading them in prayer, be sure that they vocalise their repentance, not as a form of words, but from the heart.

After teaching the Truth, I will lead in a time of silent prayer so that those present can speak from their own hearts to God. Then I will ask them to repeat a statement of faith after me, phrase by phrase. I will give an outline of these prayers in the following chapters. These should not be used as a set form or formula; I include them to show the kind of ground that is covered. Each situation is unique and you need to follow the leading of the Holy Spirit on each occasion.

In the name of Jesus and by the power of His blood, I renounce all self-deception. I ask the Holy Spirit to convict me of sin that I may not be blind to things in my life that oppose the Truth.

I choose to humble myself before God that I will not have exalted ideas about myself. I submit my mind to be instructed by the Spirit of Truth. With my mouth I intend to speak the Truth, not negatively about myself or others. I intend to live the Word of God, not only hear it.

Heavenly Father, I ask for the help of your Holy Spirit to enable me to walk in the Truth, not in self-deception.

I believe Satan no longer has any foothold in my life and cannot accuse me for my past failures. I am free, for Jesus has set me free!

In the name of Jesus and by the power of His blood I renounce every way in which I have allowed the enemy to deceive me.

I stand against any false ideas of God, the Lord Jesus Christ or the Holy Spirit.

I stand against any way in which I have been influenced by false prophecy, or by allowing others to speak untrue or deceptive words into my life.

I stand against the influence of all false teaching I have received. I forgive those who have taught me things opposed to the Truth; I pray for them, that their eyes and hearts may be opened to the Truth.

I choose to submit myself afresh to the Truth of God's Word, to be led and guided by the Spirit of Truth.

In the name of Jesus I take authority over every lying or deceiving spirit that has sought to have any influence on my life. I tell all such spirits that they have no hold whatsoever over me, or what I believe or think. I am free because Jesus Christ has set me free. To Him belongs all the glory.

In the name of Jesus and by the power of His blood, I renounce every counterfeit activity of the enemy; all influence there has been in my life through involvement with the occult, with false religions or cults. I renounce (Freemasonry, yoga or whatever may be appropriate) and I praise God that I am now free from the influence of all these activities. I renounce all superstition.

Heavenly Father, I thank you that your Holy Spirit of Truth will keep me walking in the Truth of your Word and I yield myself afresh to you; thanking you for your love and grace in bringing me out of darkness into your glorious light.

20 Dealing with Rebellion and Pride

Rebellion is deliberate – and often persistent – disobedience to the Word of the Lord and always leads to spiritual bondage.

Only genuine repentance will end the rebellion. But times of rebellion give the enemy advantages he is swift to accept.

> For rebellion is like the sin of divination, and arrogance like the evil of idolatry (1 Sam. 15:23).

No born-again Christian would willingly involve himself in witchcraft; such a thought would be unthinkable. And yet rebellion is regarded as being just as serious by the Lord.

Neither would most Christians evaluate stubborn independence as idolatry. You even hear some say, 'I value my independence'!

Satan, as Lucifer, rebelled when in heaven. He deceived Eve and then Adam rebelled, and the whole of mankind was infected with his sin. For acting independently of God's Word, both were thrown out of the garden.

Both rebellion and independence play straight into the enemy's hands. It is for these Satan was thrown out of heaven, and Adam and Eve from the garden.

Because of His mercy the Lord does not throw us out of His

Kingdom when we sin deliberately against Him. However sin yields ground to Satan, and that ground has to be retaken.

In some ways the Christian life is like climbing a mountain with the Lord. Each step takes us nearer the summit. Rebellion and independence cause us to slip down the mountain; and we continue to slip until we repent and rebellion ceases. We then start to climb again but have to retake the ground that has been lost. Although God forgives our sins, this does not mean that we are immediately restored to the same place we enjoyed before the rebellion.

The Lord certainly wants us back, and even higher up the mountain. Once again we have to devote ourselves to prayer and the Word of God and walk in obedience to regain the ground lost.

It is dangerous to look back when you are climbing; you need to be watchful as to where to place your next step. It is wonderful that God 'keeps us from falling' and will present us blameless before the throne of grace. However, Christians always regret the time wasted and the ground lost when they have departed from God's best purposes by choosing some independent way of their own.

Rebellion is not always obvious to those guilty of it. Some feel justified in having independent attitudes, and strongly self-willed people are usually reluctant to describe their attitudes as rebellious.

Stubborn refusal to accept what God says and act upon His Word is nothing less than rebellion, no matter what reasons or excuses are used by the guilty one to excuse his behaviour.

God places us under human authorities, and it is clear that He expects us to respect His authority as expressed through these human agencies. Any human expression of authority is bound to be imperfect at the very best! It is hardly surprising that so many find it more difficult to submit to others than they do directly to the Lord.

God does not call us to be one-man churches! He makes believers members of His body and teaches them to submit to

one another as well as to the Head, Christ. Such submission
involves a recognition of our interdependence, that we belong
one to another.

LEADERS

However, although He expects submission to the human
leadership in the Church, this does not give that leadership
license to 'lord it over' people 'like the Gentiles' (Matt. 20:25).
Yet there are frequent abuses of this leadership, both within
denominational structures and in some new churches.

Biblical leadership is by example. A true spiritual leader is
submitted to the leadership of the Holy Spirit in his own life
(soul submitted to Spirit) so that he can lead others – not
dominate them. His commission from God is to make responsible disciples, those who willingly submit themselves to the
Lord, not servile people who do not think for themselves and
who are prevented from making the important decisions which
are an essential part of their personal response to the Lord.

This means that every Christian should place himself under
true spiritual authority; not man-made authoritarianism
which is the fleshly substitute for the real thing. Under proper
teaching and leadership the individual believer's ministry will
develop and prosper.

The believer is also to submit to the civil government,
parents, husbands, employers, as well as to church leaders.
This is not the place to go into a lengthy discussion on each of
these areas of submission. **Any true submission comes from a
right heart attitude towards others; while rebellion and independence indicate a wrong, self-centred attitude.**

We are urged to pray for those who lead us:

Remember your leaders, who spoke the word of God to
you. Consider the outcome of their way of life and imitate
their faith. Jesus Christ is the same yesterday and today and
for ever (Heb. 13:7–8).

It is interesting to see that the statement about Jesus always being the same is made immediately after being urged to pray for our spiritual leaders. Notice what is said about these leaders:

1 **They speak the Word of God.** They lead and guide people in the way of truth.
2 **Their lives are an obvious demonstration of that truth.**
3 **You see at work in them a faith that is to be imitated.** They are fine examples of faith.
4 **They radiate faith in the Jesus who is the same today as yesterday!** You see something of the real Jesus in them, in the things they say and do, and in the fruit of their ministries.

Follow those who preach and live the truth and beware of the warning: 'Do not be carried away by all kinds of strange teachings' (Heb. 13:9).

It is not rebellion to leave a church where you are being neither led nor fed; it is common sense. In fact it could be construed as rebellion against God's Word to stay there, for you cannot grow spiritually unless you are being fed on a diet of truth; and you are not being properly led unless those in charge are going where the Holy Spirit is directing! God calls you to be fruitful, for in this He will be glorified. He will not be glorified by your remaining loyal to tradition but unfruitful at the same time.

True submission is not servility. Humility is not being humiliated.

PRIDE

Behind both rebellion and independence lies pride. Paul tells us to put *no* confidence in the flesh (Phil. 3:3). And Jesus says:

Apart from me you can do nothing (John 15:5).

Both James and Peter quote Proverbs 3:34:

> God opposes the proud but gives grace to the humble (Jas. 4:6; 1 Pet. 5:5).

We have seen the need throughout this book to keep the soul submitted to the Spirit; otherwise it will rise up in self-righteousness. This may be expressed in pride, selfishness or unbelief – or a combination of all three because clearly they work together against the best interests of the disciple.

'Humble yourselves before the Lord,' says James (4:10). It is necessary to keep the self-life humbled before God. Every believer has to do this for himself; no one else can do it for him. Only through Jesus is it possible to have a personal relationship with God. Yet this inevitably produces responsibilities for the disciple. It is for him to walk with the Lord. And if he allows pride to assert itself, he will find himself in opposition to God, not walking with Him!

If God opposes the proud, then pride obviously gives the devil opportunity. He can work with readiness on the one who centres on self, instead of denying self.

Peter echoes James in his letter:

> Humble yourselves, therefore, under God's mighty hand, that he may lift you up in due time. Cast all your anxiety on him because he cares for you (1 Pet. 5:6–7).

To hold on to anxiety is to say that you intend to bear the burden and work things out for yourself when, in reality, Jesus took your burdens on Himself and His desire is for you to live by faith in Him. It is a form of pride to depend on self instead of God!

Peter continues by warning his readers: 'Be self-controlled and alert' (v.8). That self-life must be kept under control because the devil is prowling around waiting to take advantage; and we must be alert to his intentions.

Pride goes before destruction, a haughty spirit before a fall (Prov. 16:18).

We are told to 'give no opportunity to the devil' (1 Tim. 5:14). Pride does precisely that and makes the person vulnerable to his attacks. You cannot walk on the highway of holiness in pride!

This pride takes one of two forms. **There is the aggressive, self-assertive haughtiness where one person wants to exalt himself above others.** This is readily recognised as pride and is resented by others.

However, **there is a negative introverted pride that is usually not recognised for what it is, but is equally destructive to the Christian's well-being and also has a negative effect on those around him.** This is the kind of self-assertiveness that says: 'I am no good. I am a failure. I am not sure that anyone really loves me, or accepts me. I don't expect too much of God. I want to take a back seat. I don't want to push myself forward.'

And yet that is the very thing such people are doing; they are pushing their self-life forward. And a very negative self-life at that! Their words convey what goes on in their hearts. 'I' and 'me' pepper the statements they make. Their protestations about their humility leave you unconvinced.

As we have already seen, such attitudes are negative unbelief and show an absence of real faith in what Jesus has accomplished for them. **Their attitude is as full of pride and self-centredness as the one who is self-assertive.** Behind both aspects of pride there is the obvious fact that 'self' is still to the fore and very much in control. It is simply that the two kinds of people have a different kind of self-life, both equally destructive to their well-being.

True brokenness is needed in both cases, a dying to self in order that they may be brought to faith and liberty in God's Word.

While the assertive personality elicits no sympathy from others, the danger is that the negative ones trade on it! This

only adds to their problems because it confirms them in their self-centredness.

In either case the enemy has ground on which to stand and someone through whom he can readily work. Through the self-assertive one he will walk all over other people, crushing and bruising them. Through the introverted one, he spreads self-centred, negative unbelief to anyone who will listen.

The answer in either case is obvious: repentance and a true faith in the finished work of Jesus Christ. The question is how to bring them to that point. **You cannot make another person repent, neither can you work humility in his heart. This has to be the work of the Holy Spirit.** You can only seek to be His instrument in bringing that word which will be as the hammer that breaks the rock of their hard hearts, or the double-edged sword that cuts to the division of soul and spirit, that 'judges the thoughts and attitudes of the heart'.

The introverted one has a heart that is hardened against the Truth, as does the extrovert one! **Both prefer 'self' to the truth.** And both need that word from God that will penetrate their shells of self-protectiveness.

What is most serious is that there is a clash of wills between God and the individual. In both cases, **they do not want to let go of self.** They may hate themselves for what they are, and yet still cling to self. They fear losing their identity, and so cannot find their true identity in Christ.

Before either has the breakthrough needed, there will have to be a renunciation of self, a releasing of themselves to God. They will need to learn what it truly means to live for others and not themselves. Even their service of others has centred around self, wanting to prove their abilities on the one hand, or desiring recognition and praise to build up self-esteem on the other.

Either can be manipulative and so seek to exercise control over others. This is an opening for a real work of the enemy, as **a spirit of control is one of the most subtle and invidious of his activities among Christians.**

The proud extroverts exercise control by lording it over others; they use people for their own personal ends and to further their own ministries. They often treat people with disdain, are highly critical and take no notice of the scriptural instruction to count others better than yourself (Phil. 2:3). Such an idea seems to them ridiculous as they are so much wiser (in their own eyes), more capable, and everything would be done more quickly and with better results if only others listened to them and did as they were told!

It is the strong streak of independence, often coupled with considerable natural abilities, that makes it difficult for such people to be willing to deny self, to be broken before the Lord and therefore before others. Once this process has taken place, however, they can be mighty in God's purposes.

Saul of Tarsus was full of self-righteous zeal, convinced that he was serving God by persecuting the Church. No doubt he had listened to many testimonies from believers he had arrested, proclaiming Jesus to be the Christ; but he vigorously held on to his own religious views.

Yet once broken before the Lord he became Paul, the mighty apostle. Three days of blindness to show him how blind he had been, and several years in obscurity to prepare him for the ministry God had purposed for him! He could not have become the man of God he became without this breaking process, learning what it meant to lose self, rather than serve God with the mistaken zeal and self-righteous pride of the self or soul life.

It is equally difficult and costly, but in a different way, for those with a low self-image to lose self. **A spirit of control works through them, because the enemy can so easily control them. They are manipulative because they are readily manipulated by him.**

They are eager to get their own way, and will go to great lengths to obtain what they want. They manipulate others by using their time to talk endlessly about themselves and their problems. They accuse others of lacking love for them if they do not give them what they want. They often seem so considerate and loving, yet always seem to end up getting what they want – their own way! They can be very pleasant but you find yourself manipulated into doing what they want.

Such people are often very capable, but feel the need to have their abilities recognised by others. They appear easily hurt when they do not receive the thanks and acclaim they desire.

They are certainly self-deceived for they do not recognise their pride. They think of themselves as quite the opposite. Some of them see themselves as humble, others hate themselves for being so introverted and giving in to so many fears. They manipulate because they are convinced that others would not notice them or love them unless they manipulated their love. This is the pattern of life and relationships they have experienced over a lifetime; so the pattern is not always easy to break.

Once again, such believers need to encounter the truth, rather than simply have an experience of God's power. For it is only the revelation of the truth that will make them aware of their need; only the Holy Spirit can bring them the necessary conviction! **They need to see how they have allowed the enemy to manipulate and control them, and then stand against him.** You can pray and agree with them once they are prepared to acknowledge their need and renounce the way they have been manipulated and have sought to control others.

In humbling himself before God, the proud extrovert has to come to a heart knowledge that his flesh counts for nothing, that all he does apart from Jesus, that is not initiated and empowered by the Holy Spirit, is worth nothing. As he has spent a lifetime exalting his self-life he is going to experience much refining as he discovers what it means to 'deny himself, take up his cross and follow' Jesus. Only then can he understand his true position in Christ.

Often, while the process takes place, it seems to him that everything is falling apart. Whatever he puts his hand to goes wrong; in the past he was so capable while things were in his hands! But he will only discover the real power of the Holy Spirit in his life as he learns to depend on the Lord.

To tell the proud introvert that he needs to repent might meet with a response of astonishment, for he has such a low opinion of self he could not see what else there is to repent about. To him it seems he is always repenting.

Because of their insecurities the introverts feel they have to do everything possible to keep hold of what little self-respect they have, instead of letting go and discovering their true identity in Christ. They are afraid of a total loss of identity.

Many people go through a period when they appear to fluctuate between living in revelation of the new, and sinking back into the old ways of thinking and behaving. They want to believe the truth, but feel weighed down and pulled back by the old.

We need to stand in faith with them, standing firm against the devices of the enemy who wants them to stay bound by their old ways of thinking so that they cannot enjoy their inheritance in Christ or be fruitful for God. He would prefer them to stay bound, not to be released into freedom, and to continue to spread negativity and unbelief all around them. He must not be allowed to have his way.

CONFRONTATION

To help either the proud extrovert or the proud introvert, confrontation will be necessary. And these are not easy people to confront, which is why they have persisted in their manipulative behaviour for so long.

The one seeking to help either will need to be bold but in differing ways, for the extrovert and introvert cannot be treated in the same way because their personalities are so different. However, without strong confrontation they are unlikely to face their need.

Jesus was very confrontational in His style of ministry and we can learn much from Him in this. The reason for this is simple: **the Truth is confrontational by its very nature.** Light and darkness are utterly opposed to one another, as is the flesh to the Spirit. They are completely at odds. So if people are living in the flesh (and often imagining they are being spiritual) their deception has to be exposed. You are unlikely to receive many thanks for doing this. Such people will only be thankful when they come to a revelation of the truth that sets them free from the control that has operated through them.

The proud extrovert is likely to dismiss what you say; the introvert will suggest you cannot understand him!

It is important not to be deflected from your purpose, no matter what reaction you receive. You want to see these people set free, not persist in their bondage. And you must be prepared to love them, no matter what the cost to yourself. The extrovert will try to crush you and make you feel stupid; the introvert will accuse and try to make you feel insensitive and unloving. Remember both groups have had plenty of practice!

However the Truth is able to set anyone free. The cross is the power of God's salvation or healing to anyone who believes!

It is difficult to persist when those you try to help do everything possible to make you think you are wrong in your estimate of the situation and your approach to it. In love, persist and show them that you will not be shaken by their tactics. If they threaten not to have any more to do with you, do not pander to them. That is precisely what they want. They may threaten not to have any more to do with you, but if you have spoken a word of truth to them pray that the Holy Spirit will 'water' the seed you have sown. In nearly every case they will return and with a different attitude, more open to the Truth and therefore to the help you can give them.

And don't be too discouraged when people seem to be making good progress and then regress, at least temporarily. This is common. You are responsible for speaking the truth in love, but you cannot hold yourself responsible for the way in which others respond to that truth.

PRAYER AND FAITH DECLARATION

In the name of Jesus and by the power of His blood I renounce all rebellion and pride, and every way in which I have allowed the enemy to influence my life through my rebellious and proud attitudes. I renounce all my independent and self-sufficient attitudes, every way in which I have opposed the teaching of God's Word and have failed to put my trust and confidence in Him.

I renounce the spirit of control, every way in which I have allowed my life to be controlled or manipulated by others. And I stand against any such spirit of control being able to operate through my life to influence others.

I forgive those leaders who have sought to control me, and I pray that they will become men of true spiritual authority.

I renounce my aggressive, self-assertive pride, all self-centredness, every way in which I have tried to elicit sympathy and pity from others. I renounce all self-centredness and rejoice that the old has gone and the new has come, that I have died and my life is now hidden with Christ in God.

Heavenly Father, I thank you that you have forgiven me for every way in which I have spoken negatively of myself, denying my inheritance in Christ. Again I submit myself to the Truth that I may live in freedom from self, and all the influence of the false accuser. I praise you that you always lead me in triumph in Christ. Hallelujah!

21 Unforgiveness

We have already seen how important it is to forgive those who have caused past hurts, to be in a right attitude towards all who have affected our lives negatively. However, we also have need of ongoing forgiveness. Jesus said:

> For if you forgive men when they sin against you, your heavenly Father will also forgive you. But if you do not forgive men their sins, your Father will not forgive your sins (Matt. 6:14–15).

Refusal to forgive others puts you outside God's forgiveness, and that is serious! To be in a state of unforgiveness before God is to be in rebellion against Him, and this will inevitably hinder the flow of His provision and power in the believer's life. It is clear from the parable Jesus teaches that **the unmerciful servant's refusal to forgive the debt of his fellow servant resulted in his return to the bondage, out of which his master had taken him:**

> Then the master called the servant in. 'You wicked servant', he said, 'I cancelled all that debt of yours because you begged me to. Shouldn't you have had mercy on your

fellow-servant just as I had on you?' In anger his master turned him over to the jailers . . . until he should pay back all he owed. 'This is how my heavenly Father will treat each of you unless you forgive your brother from your heart' (Matt. 18:32-5).

These are strong words and demonstrate how essential it is to be merciful. 'Blessed are the merciful, for they will be shown mercy' (Matt. 5:7).

God wants us to be merciful so that our immediate response when others fail, hurt or offend us is to forgive them. Satan of course will do anything possible to stir up feelings of bitterness, anger and resentment. He knows God's Word. He knows that failure to forgive will make you vulnerable to his devices; so it is understandable that he will use every argument he can to persuade you not to forgive:

'Why should you forgive? The other was in the wrong.'
'You cannot forgive until he comes and asks for forgiveness.'
'It is for him to come to you to be reconciled; it is not for you to go to him.'
'It is too easy to forgive such a great hurt. He should be made to suffer first.'
'He deserves to be punished for what he did to you.'

Such are the statements of the father of lies! They appeal to the flesh, but utterly oppose the truth Jesus teaches us. No ground should be yielded to the enemy here.

Bitterness and resentment give him a foothold in a person's thinking and enable him to encourage feelings of self-righteousness, condemnation and self-pity (which is like a spiritual cancer that eats away within a person's soul).

Many who know there is no condemnation for them because they are in Christ Jesus, frequently have to fight feelings of condemnation. One of the chief reasons for this is that they condemn others, and so reap what they sow.

Do not judge, or you too will be judged. For in the same way as you judge others, you will be judged, and with the measure you use, it will be measured to you (Matt. 7:1–2).

Jesus then teaches the parable about looking at the speck of sawdust in your brother's eye, while you have a plank in your own! Your problem is greater because you have a wrong heart attitude towards the one who has offended you. If it seems right to point out the sin to your brother (Matt. 18:15), this needs to be done in love, not judgment. The aim is to be reconciled with him, not to judge or condemn him.

If his sin is deliberate because he has a wrong heart attitude then God alone can deal with him. This is no reason to condone a wrong heart attitude on your own part! Two wrongs don't make a right!

Forgiveness is a decision, not a feeling.

We live in a world where most live for themselves and Jesus warned that in it we would experience tribulation. There will be those who think nothing of defrauding and cheating you, lying, deceiving, falsely accusing, ridiculing you for your faith, taking advantage of you, and so on. The enemy working through human agents!

It is more hurtful when other Christians treat you like this; you would not expect them to be used by the enemy in such ways. Sometimes you are left wondering who you can trust!

Your own sinful attitudes or lack of wisdom may be a significant part of the total picture. So it is necessary to acknowledge before God the ways in which, even inadvertently, you have contributed to the problem. And then **you have to forgive, no matter how deep the hurts or how prolonged and persistent the sin against you.**

Then Peter came to Jesus and asked, 'Lord, how many times shall I forgive my brother when he sins against me? Up to seven times?' Jesus answered, 'I tell you, not seven times, but seventy-seven times' (Matt. 18:21–2).

This is the Gospel! **It is good news to know that the Lord has completely forgiven you! It is equally good news to know that you are to forgive!** Failure to do so will result in further pain for you and disruption of your peace, which will affect your walk with God; and He wants to spare you that!

> If your brother sins, rebuke him, and if he repents, forgive him. If he sins against you seven times in a day, and seven times comes back to you and says, 'I repent,' forgive him (Luke 17:3–4).

It would seem that someone such as this is lacking in genuine repentance if he keeps returning to the same sin; and yet Jesus says you are to forgive him. There is no alternative. After all this is how we often treat the Lord. We say we are sorry and ask Him to forgive a particular sin. We are determined not to repeat the sin, and yet find that it is not long before we are back before Him confessing the same thing again.

Was the confession of sin sincere in the first place? Oh yes. **But the sin persisted because the heart had not experienced change. The Lord will give you the change of heart once that is what you genuinely want.**

As we have seen, there is nothing you can do effectively to change another person's heart. You can ensure that your heart is right, full of mercy, love and grace.

Jesus teaches us the 'golden rule': 'Do to others what you would have them do to you' (Matt. 7:12). It is fatal to retaliate when others wrong you:

> Do not repay anyone evil for evil. Be careful to do what is right in the eyes of everybody. If it is possible, as far as it depends on you, live at peace with everyone. Do not take revenge, my friends, but leave room for God's wrath, for it is written: 'It is mine to avenge; I will repay,' says the Lord. On the contrary: 'If your enemy is hungry, feed him; if he is thirsty, give him something to drink. In doing this, you will

heap burning coals on his head.' Do not be overcome by evil, but overcome evil with good (Rom. 12:17–21).

Judgment is the Lord's prerogative, not yours! The love Jesus expects among His disciples is expressed in forgiving so completely that you pray for your enemy, feed him, give him something to drink!

Stand against the enemy's attempts to dredge up hurts. Sometimes certain events set off a chain-reaction within you, and old feelings of bitterness begin to rise up within you. In such circumstances it is good to say (aloud if you are in a suitable place) that all that pertains to those events is completely forgiven and is 'under the blood' of Jesus. He does not dredge up your sins, so don't allow the enemy to do so.

It is important to claim back from the enemy any ground that has been lost through unforgiveness. **When you forgive immediately, you have not lost any ground; in fact you have gained it.** Your immediate soul-reaction may be one of dismay to the events that have taken place; if you are living submitted to the Spirit, He will give you the grace to forgive immediately. Your faith has proved genuine in the crisis, and you have gained ground. We have already seen that we only have to retake ground we lose to the enemy. So it is best not to lose it!

The flesh does not like to forgive and will try to justify your reaction of outrage at the offence against you. If this fleshly reaction is not checked immediately it will gain a tighter grasp on you. You will get to the point where you know it is wrong, but feel powerless to react in any other way.

A jealous person does not want to be jealous, feels resentful towards the one causing the jealousy (as he sees the situation), but feels unable to rid himself of the jealousy. This is an emotional bondage which may involve needing to forgive others; but the jealous person has to acknowledge that the real problem is within himself. **'Nothing outside a man can defile a man', says Jesus. He is defiled by what is in his own heart.** So it would be wrong for him to accuse others for being the cause of his jealousy, even if someone has done something to trigger off this reaction within him.

When falsely accused, be like Jesus at His trial; say nothing! Do not seek to justify yourself before God or man. Forgive and be thankful that God is so merciful to you! Seek 'to live at peace with everyone'. Live a life of forgiveness.

Sometimes a person seeking counsel will claim: 'I can't forgive.' This is not true. What the person really means is, 'I don't feel it is right to forgive, and therefore I won't.'

The person will remain in bondage to the offender until he does forgive. He also places himself in bondage to the enemy. Encourage him to face his need to forgive, and to tell the Lord that he specifically forgives X for doing 'such and such' to him. He needs to be specific, to vocalise who he is forgiving and for what. Just as he is thankful that his own sins are under the blood, never to be held against him, so he is to regard the offences he forgives in a similar light.

The test of forgiveness is to be able to treat the offender with love, as if the offence had never taken place. This is the outworking of God's grace. He has given us:

the ministry of reconciliation: that God was reconciling the world to himself in Christ, not counting men's sins against them (2 Cor. 5:18–19).

It is a vital part of reconciliation that you do not count others' sins against them, no matter how difficult that might seem at first!

PRAYER AND FAITH DECLARATION

Heavenly Father I thank you for your mercy and grace, that you have forgiven all my sins and cleansed me from all unrighteousness. I praise you for the victory of the blood and cross of Jesus, and that I can now live the new life in the power of your Spirit.

In the name of Jesus and by the power of His blood I choose to forgive all who have ever sinned against me, those who have rejected me or hurt me in any way, those who have opposed me or spoken ill of me. And I pray that every one of them will know the forgiveness of Jesus Christ and His acceptance.

In particular I choose to forgive N . . . for . . . I thank you, Heavenly Father, that you have forgiven me for all the negative attitudes I have had towards these events and those who caused them. I thank you that I am now set free from all harmful and negative influences these events have had on my life. And I thank you, Father, that the enemy cannot have any advantage over me now because of these things. I am free from all the hurt and from the influence of those who have caused it. My past is behind me. Now I can walk into the future with confidence, with a believing, forgiving heart, rejoicing in your love and mercy.

22   Strongholds and Curses

The enemy's purpose is to try to place Christians in bondage. He has no right to do this, and cannot succeed without the believer's co-operation, however inadvertently that is given.

The enemy is the tempter. You can only be tempted in an area where your flesh enjoys the enticements offered you. So what might tempt one Christian will not necessarily tempt another.

Bondage occurs when a believer yields persistently to a particular temptation so that a pattern of sin is established in his life. It is easy to recognise these bondages in others; so we need to avoid judging them and seek to restore those who fall into serious sin (Gal. 6:1). You can be thankful that by God's grace you have not fallen into that sin; but at the same time be sure that the enemy is not being allowed to have victory in your life in some other way!

Most Christians have to face the problem of habitual sin at some time. They will try to keep these sins secret. Yet their very presence leads to internal conflict which will seriously hinder the person's witness. This is often the problem in Christians who show great potential and yet never seem to realise that potential. Others cannot see what God sees. He knows what hinders the fulfilment of His purpose.

Struggling with an area of persistent sin causes many a believer to think of himself as a failure. He sees himself as weak, and feels a hypocrite for appearing to be different externally from what he knows himself to be internally.

There can be two main causes for habitual sin. **The believer continues to be tempted in a particular way because he does not truly want to be set free in that area.** He enjoys that particular sin; it appeals to his flesh and satisfies his soul in the wrong way.

His enjoyment of the sin produces further conflict. He may try to justify the sin as part of God's will for him. The heart can be very deceptive!

Alternatively, he knows clearly that the sin he enjoys is sin, and he hates himself for liking it. This produces further conflict within him. Part of him wants to be set free from this; another part doesn't. If only he didn't enjoy this sin it would be so much easier!

He confesses the sin to God, yet knows in his heart of hearts that he will commit the same offence again and will need to come back to the Lord for further forgiveness. While this process is going on it seems he is treading water spiritually. He can put much effort into his activities without making any noticeable progress. It seems there is little anointing or fruit in his Christian life.

All this serves the enemy's purposes, for he does not want the believer to make progress!

The other cause for this persistent sin is that for some reason the enemy may have had the opportunity to place this believer in bondage. It could be that this sin has become such a habit, the Christian feels powerless to oppose it.

Sin invites demonic attack. Take obvious examples such as lust or greed. The believer knows his lust is wrong but enjoys his lustful fantasies, reads the wrong magazines and watches the wrong videos or movies. He wants to walk with the Lord, but this is his area of weakness. Self-effort has proved futile; he keeps returning to the very things that feed the lust.

The enemy is good at putting the wrong materials before

him. He feeds lustful thoughts which affect the way he views the opposite sex (or the same sex in the case of those in homosexual bondage). He feels overcome. He asks for ministry, believing that he needs to be delivered from a demon of lust that has him in its grip.

This may well be the case, but it is a problem of his own making. It is possible for you to rebuke the demon and he will have to retreat, which will give the believer temporary relief; but unless the heart of the matter is dealt with, the problem or bondage will inevitably return.

A CHANGE OF HEART

There has to be a change of heart. For that to take place, the Christian must want the change of heart that only God can give him. He will need to desire genuinely the purity of heart and mind God wants him to have.

Without such a change of heart, the desire for the sin will remain; and he will struggle constantly, fearing further failure. With a change of heart the problem disappears. However, knowing his former weakness, he will be wise not to place himself in a position of temptation again. He is like a former alcoholic who learns to refuse alcoholic beverage. One drink could begin a slippery slide downwards again.

The example given of lust is true of any sin: greed, criticism, judgment, jealousy, etc.

The one who is persistently critical feels justified in his critical attitudes towards others and often does not recognise his sin. His persistent sin places him in bondage to critical spirits who are able to work through him to hinder and destroy others. Such a believer may be oblivious to the way the enemy is manipulating and using him.

When people cannot break free from such bondage, they often need to confess their sin to another and have someone stand with them against the enemy. It is not easy to stand alone against the very spirits you have attracted by your behaviour! However, a change of heart alters the ground on which they stand and their ability to withstand the enemy's devices.

Overcoming the enemy is a question of authority. A Christian will only be able to speak with authority to unclean spirits, of whatever kind, if he does not want the sin with which they try to entice him. Peter urges us to 'abstain from sinful desires, which war against your soul' (1 Pet. 2:11). The nature of the flesh never changes. Your flesh will always be enticed by sin, which is why it is so important to walk in the Spirit.

While the soul is submitted to the Spirit, the good things of the Holy Spirit flood through the soul. When filled with love for Jesus, there is little room for love of self; when the Spirit is flowing freely in your life, it is much easier to walk in the Spirit, and so give no room for the flesh:

> I say then: Walk in the Spirit, and you shall not fulfil the lust of the flesh. For the flesh lusts against the Spirit, and the Spirit against the flesh; and these are contrary to one another, so that you do not do the things that you wish (Gal. 5:16–17 NKJ).

> But put on the Lord Jesus Christ, and make no provision for the flesh, to fulfil its lusts (Rom. 13:14 NKJ).

Prevention is better than cure! Jesus Christ has set us free. So Paul advises:

> Stand firm, then, and do not let yourselves be burdened again by a yoke of slavery (Gal. 5:1).

You are yoked to Jesus and are no longer a slave to sin. It is never true for a Christian to say: 'I couldn't help it', when referring to his failure to resist temptation. **God will not allow us to be tempted beyond our ability to endure and always provides the escape route!** (1 Cor. 10:13).

Jesus has set you free to enable you to serve others in love and thus express your love for Him, not indulge the flesh (Gal. 5:13). Sin is by nature deceptive. It is the devil's lie that it will bring happiness and fulfilment. He suggests that to yield the heart to God so that the root of sin is dealt with would lead only to a sense of loss.

The opposite is the truth; for it is only submission to the Lord that will bring the release and freedom the believer wants. **A change of heart brings a change of desire.** You do not miss what you do not want! The mind set on what the Spirit desires is life and peace.

PERSONAL REVIVAL

Many Christians subject themselves to unnecessary torture and defeat over long periods of time through their failure to face the real issues, come before God and begin crying out to Him for the change of heart needed.

You can help by standing with a believer against his bondages, but remember this will be futile without his co-operation. It is for him to seek the change of heart he needs.

It is very helpful to be part of a body of believers who have the same aim; they want to live in personal revival, to glorify Jesus, to walk in the Spirit in ways that please the Lord. For by seeking God together many of these heart issues are addressed, because of the depth of the repentance taking place corporately.

In times of revival God challenges His children to face the need of practical holiness in their lives. They have to face honestly those areas of their lives which are a denial of being Christlike. As God works this sanctity in them, the holiness of God's people challenges the unholiness that exists in churches and in the world around. The holy people of God become leaven in the lump, light for the world and salt for the earth.

Then the nations will know that I am the Lord, declares the Sovereign Lord, **when I show myself holy through you before their eyes** (Ezek. 36:23).

Revival is the fruit that results from the way God dealt personally with the hearts of His children.

STRONGHOLDS

God has given believers every spiritual weapon they need to overcome the enemy.

The weapons we fight with are not the weapons of the world. On the contrary, **they have divine power to demolish strongholds.** We demolish arguments and every pretension that sets itself up against the knowledge of God, and we take captive every thought to make it obedient to Christ (2 Cor. 10:4–5).

God transforms us into His likeness by the renewing of our minds. It is important that the enemy is not allowed to retain a 'stronghold' in a believer's thought life, an area of thinking inconsistent with the Truth of His Word. You could describe a stronghold as a wrong pattern of thought that has a considerable influence on the person, perhaps of criticism, anger, jealousy or lust.

Such 'strongholds' are often the aftermath of years of wrong thinking before being converted to Christ. At new birth the Christian's attitudes towards several areas of his life would have changed immediately; but he did not become instantaneously perfect! God's refining purposes continue within him. And part of that purpose is to rid his mind of any enemy strongholds.

Sometimes these are of a religious nature. Holding on to traditions, religious prejudice or denominational thinking is evidence of enemy strongholds. These result in resistance to change and unbelief. People will prefer their own thoughts to the Truth!

If the heart is full of truth, the person's thinking will be right. A stronghold in the mind resists the Truth, so must be pulled down, using the spiritual weapons God has provided.

Again the believer has to stand against these strongholds himself after facing the fact that they are present and are wrong. Unless his thinking is right, neither his speech nor actions will be as God intends. We have the authority 'to demolish arguments and every pretension that sets itself up against the knowledge of God'.

We have seen how important it is that the believer's heart is right with God, that he feeds on the Truth, 'eating' the Bread of Life, the Living Word that comes down from heaven. This will correct any of his wrong ideas or opinions.

And he will need to learn to reject immediately any thought that is a contradiction to God's Word. If he receives one negative, the enemy will follow that with another, and then another. Before long he will have been allowed to establish another stronghold of negative thinking which will have to be dealt with.

CURSES

It is, however, possible for Christians to experience an oppressive heaviness for which they can find no rational account. Things can go wrong, and apparently for no reason. They may realise that this is enemy opposition but do not know how to deal with it.

The Lord has put before us the way of blessing or the way of curse:

This day I call heaven and earth as witnesses against you that I have set before you life and death, blessings and curses. Now choose life, so that you and your children may live and that you may love the Lord your God, listen to his voice, and hold fast to him. For the Lord is your life, and he will give you many years in the land he swore to give to your fathers, Abraham, Isaac and Jacob (Deut. 30:19–20).

Again the Lord emphasises how important it is to walk in the Truth, to obey His Word and so inherit the promises He gives us.

In reality many Christians curse themselves, obviously without intending to do so. **They do this by speaking of themselves in ways which deny what God says about them, when they choose to disobey, when they are guilty of unbelief instead of walking by faith.**

Some, however, have been converted from families that have been under curses for generations. This is no cause for fear. Curses are easy to break because of the victory Jesus has won on the cross. The Holy Spirit is more powerful than any other spirit, and Jesus has already disarmed the principalities and powers that are against us (Col. 2:15). We have the authority to break the power of any curse that stands against us.

When the believer breaks the power of a curse over his family, other members of the wider family are also set free, even if they are not themselves believers.

A believer is able to exercise faith to overcome hereditary disease. His inheritance now comes from above, not from former generations. It is not the Lord's purpose for him to live in fear of sickness, or in fear of communicating sickness to his children. With new life in Christ the curse can be cut off and cancelled.

The curse of the fallen nature is carried on from one generation to another. Christian parents can begin to pray for their children while still in the womb, and from birth they can enfold them in the love of Jesus and teach them the Truth. Their children can come to a saving knowledge of Jesus at an early age. The curse of Adam is then replaced by the blessing of Christ's living presence within!

Demonic strongholds have persisted in some families through the sin of former generations. For example, there may be a history of suicides in several past generations. The power of Jesus's blood is able to save the believer from such demonic activity. The believer can renounce the sin of their ancestors that caused the problem initially, and break the power of the curses that have resulted.

Other members of the family may 'pray' for them by invoking occult powers through involvement with spiritism, a cult or false religion. The believer need not fear; he has God's armour and protection.

However he would be wise to move on to the attack by binding the evil powers that are being invoked, and by praying for those family members involved. This is sometimes of great importance in a case of serious sickness. A spiritual battle can take place if the believer is calling on God, while others are calling demonic powers to influence the same situation.

Satan has no claim over one who has been purchased for God with the blood of Jesus. God's purpose for every believer is blessing not curse, that:

From the fulness of his grace we have all received one blessing after another (John 1:16).

This is what God wants us *all* to receive so that we *all* overflow with blessing towards others.

Jesus bore even oppression for us so that we might be liberated from it. 'He was oppressed and afflicted' (Isa. 53:7). He became 'a curse' so that we might be delivered from the curse of legalistic religion, and be able to live in the power of His Spirit and the Truth of His Word – in freedom! (Gal. 3:13).

PRAYER AND FAITH DECLARATION

In the name of Jesus and through the victory of the cross I stand against any habitual sin in my life and the bondage that has resulted from this.

Heavenly Father, I repent of this sin (N . . .). I choose to turn away from it so that my life may no longer be under its

influence, and that I shall no longer grieve you in this way. Please forgive me for any way in which this sin has given the devil opportunity in my life, and for the ways in which my sins have influenced others negatively.

I choose to submit my heart afresh to you that you might work change in my life.

Thank you, Father, that I am yoked together with Jesus. I want to be more like Him. Change me into His likeness from one degree of glory to another.

In the name of Jesus and by the power of His blood I come against every enemy stronghold in my thinking. I have the mind of Christ, and choose to submit my thinking to the Truth of God's Word.

In particular I come against the stronghold of (Name them . . .). I now use the spiritual weapons that are mighty to the pulling down of strongholds and everything in my life which sets itself up against the knowledge of Christ. I believe those strongholds are now pulled down. I choose to submit my mind to the truth of God's Word. I will not allow any fresh strongholds of unbelief or negativity to be established in my thinking with your grace and help.

In the name of Jesus and by the power of His blood I now exercise the authority given me by Jesus Christ, and I break the power of any and every curse brought against me, or any member of the family to which I belong. The power of that curse is now broken, and I and the members of my family are delivered completely from any influence this has had on our lives.

I choose to bless all who have sought to curse me.

I praise you, Heavenly Father, that I do not need to live in any fear of the devil or future curse. You are my shield and I praise you for the victory you give me over every device of the evil one through Jesus.

PART 4

DIRECT COUNSELLING

23 Speaking into Others' Lives

Direct Counselling is just that. It is direct. It is concerned with the truth that sets people free, and aims at the heart of a person's problems.

Direct Counselling has to be centred on the revelation of God's Truth and can only be exercised in the power of the Holy Spirit, the Spirit of Truth.

THE FRUIT OF THE SPIRIT

You will need to experience the fruit of the Holy Spirit abundantly when you counsel. **These are the qualities of the Counsellor, and they need to be evident in anyone who counsels in the name of Jesus.**

Love is the first-fruit of the Holy Spirit. Without love for those you counsel your ministry to them will prove unfruitful. **Even if you speak the truth, others will find it difficult to receive what you say unless you speak the Truth in love.**

Joy You will need to maintain your joy throughout, no matter how despondent the one you are seeking to help. Even when you weep with those who weep you are drawing them to faith in God for their situation, to a place where they will **'rejoice in the Lord always'** and **'give thanks in all circumstances'**.

Peace   It is essential that you remain peaceful, no matter how agitated others become. This is a demonstration of faith in the face of difficulty. You will find no difficulty in doing this if you keep listening to the Spirit and remain in an attitude of forgiveness, no matter what you hear! **Discern, but don't judge!**
Patience   Often you will need an infinite supply of this fruit of the Spirit, especially when people are slow to respond to what God says to them. **Apart from faith in God's Word, being patient is the quality most necessary for counsellors.**
Kindness   **You will need to be a human agent of God's mercy again and again,** directing people to the truth that by His grace they are perfectly loved and made totally acceptable in His sight.
Goodness   You minister to people for their good. **So you are prepared to be confrontational if necessary,** even though you risk rejection as a result. And you want to be an example to others of the life of which you speak; that you are living in the good of what God has done for you in Christ.
Faithfulness   No matter who you are counselling, or what their problems, **you are to remain faithful to the Truth of God's Word.** It is faith in that Truth that will set them free; so you dare not depart from the Truth into reason, sentiment or emotion.
Gentleness   Even when you have to say strong things to people you will need to do so with a gentle spirit. **Jesus was very confrontational, but described Himself as 'gentle and humble in heart'.** So don't brow-beat people with the truth. Lead them into the realisation that all Jesus has done, He has done for them!
Self-control   Avoid showing facial response to what is said to you; **appear as impassive as possible.** Do not give away what you are thinking. The person may be looking to you for signs of approval, acceptance, judgment, even repulsion or rejection. **You are drawing him to Christ and His love and acceptance;** so you do not want him distracted by your reactions.

We have seen the need to depend on the spiritual gifts God has given us, especially the word of knowledge which enables us to understand the true nature of the problem, and the word of wisdom which enables us to speak the right word into the situation.

It is much better to trust the witness of the Holy Spirit who will never lie to you, than to the views of the person you are seeking to help.

In the case of a believer, the Holy Spirit within him will witness to the truth of what you say in the name of Jesus. He may smother the inner witness of the Spirit, preferring to believe his own reason or feelings. I have known it to take several months before some have been prepared to receive what God has said to them; wasted months because they were not prepared to face the Truth. But God will not change His Word for anyone. He waits patiently until he is prepared to receive and respond to His Word.

Often the perception God gives you of a person's problem is very different from the believer's own perception of his need. He will need a change of attitude before he is prepared to receive the Lord's Word into his life.

It is better to trust the way you believe the Spirit is leading you to pray and risk being wrong, than to ignore the prompting of the Spirit. If you have submitted yourself to be led by the Spirit you will seldom be mistaken, even though sometimes you will not understand why you feel moved to pray in a particular way!

On one occasion I felt moved to pray for a man to be healed of a kidney disease. He was asking for prayer for something totally different! Some time later I met him again. He told me that at the time he thought I was mistaken in the way I prayed for him, although he said nothing out of politeness. About two years later he had to have a hospital check-up for something entirely unrelated. During the course of the extensive examination he received, it was discovered that he had been living a normal life on less than half a kidney. 'You should be dead', the doctor told him, 'not walking around like this!'

220 THE TRUTH THAT SETS YOU FREE

You will certainly need to use the gift of faith, often in relation to the gifts of healings. It is worth noting that both words are in the plural. Gifts of healings are given to the Church. I would never allow anyone who claimed to have a gift of healing to pray for me. Those who minister in the occult make such claims. Those who minister in the Spirit recognise that they have the authority to heal, and God gives them the anointing to administer His healing grace to others, that they may receive gifts of healings. If the minister possessed these gifts himself he could clear the local hospital!

Not even Jesus made such a claim. He made it clear He could do nothing of Himself, but only what He saw His Father doing. He would never act independently of His Father. On occasions the power of God was present to heal the sick; so presumably even in His ministry there were occasions when the Spirit moved powerfully in this particular way.

There is little point in praying with people, laying hands on them or anointing them unless we and they expect things to happen. God will work miracles through anyone who believes (John 14:12), but the anointing of the Holy Spirit is essential. It is that anointing that makes us fruitful and successful in ministry. Those ministering submit themselves to the Spirit, then God's power can flow through their soul life and out of their bodies as rivers of living water.

We can go through the motions of ministry without anointing and not much will happen as a result. **We need anointing to speak the Truth so that people will hear God and respond,** and we need anointing to fulfil the commission to heal the sick in the name of Jesus.

When you do not see the results you need, don't blame the people to whom you are ministering; seek from Him the anointing that will break the yoke.

You will need to exercise the gift of the discerning of spirits. **It is important to discern to what degree you are coping with a situation that has arisen from someone walking in the flesh, and how much is due to enemy activity.**

When you prophesy over people, encourage them to test what is said. If you give them a major directive prophecy, show them that God will speak to them further Himself and will also confirm what is said through other witnesses.

When you pray in tongues over people, be open to receive the interpretation. Then you will be able to understand the way in which the Holy Spirit is leading you to pray. Often, you will flow easily from one to the other, tongues, interpretation, then tongues again, more interpretation, tongues, interpretation; and so on. In this way the Spirit guides the direction of your prayers and your understanding of the situation is greatly increased.

You will find that the Holy Spirit will go for the heart of the matter, not the superficial symptoms. So a person may come with a superficial request, only to find that God gives you a word that cuts to the division of soul and spirit, and tests the desires and intentions of his heart!

THE CRUNCH ISSUE

When seeking to bring someone to faith in Jesus Christ you can spend a great deal of time answering questions, parrying criticisms of the Church and the failures of some believers. The person will be no nearer the Kingdom of God as a result. There may be some vital questions to be answered; but you have to confront the person with the real issue as quickly as possible. 'Do you **want** to know Jesus?' It may be that you have to state the truth starkly. 'Your life is in a mess and only Jesus can alter that'; or to challenge boldly: 'You need to ask for God's forgiveness and surrender your life to Jesus. Are you prepared to do that?'

You may well receive a negative response. Do not always believe what you hear! It is likely that the person before you is in conflict, fearful about what will happen if he does surrender to Jesus.

On occasions I have found it right to call people's bluff: 'I don't believe that. I think you do want Jesus in your life but you are afraid of the repercussions.' On nearly every such occasion the person has admitted this is true and minutes later has come to Christ.

Jesus did not allow the woman at the well in Samaria (John 4:19) to slip off the hook by trying to initiate a discussion about the proper way to worship. He used a word of knowledge to reach her heart and her need; and her life was transformed. As a result the whole village came to hear Jesus.

This principle is true, not only in evangelism but in all counselling. **Listen to the witness of the Spirit and go for the heart.** Time and again people will try to avoid facing the real issue. **It is for you to keep the flow of conversation to the point.** You have achieved nothing if you have allowed the other person to dictate the course of the conversation by asking you questions that have been ideal openings for you to air your considerable spiritual knowledge! They have appealed to your soulish pride and have been successful!

SETTING PEOPLE FREE

Those who engage in lengthy counselling techniques often do so for their own soulish reasons. They want to be needed, to have a ministry that others will appreciate and even depend on. These are fleshly desires and are likely to lead into bondage both the one counselling and the one being counselled. When challenged about this their reactions show they do not want to 'lose their souls'; they think they have found a spiritual identity in the 'counselling ministry'. This is dangerous deception.

There are limitations to any counselling. Its purpose is to help and encourage the believer in his or her walk with God. **Counselling is not to replace that walk, or to try and find a slick alternative to discipleship.**

Imagine a person shackled to an iron ball and chain, which he is trying to drag along as he walks. How would you help him? Would you suggest that he turns round and counts the links on the chain? Or that he goes and examines the ball to discern its contents? Or that he discusses what the ball consists of, or how it could be lifted? Obviously not!

You would simply unshackle him at the ankle and let him go free! That is precisely the effect that Direct Counselling has. The truth unshackles a person and sets him free.

THE AIMS OF DIRECT COUNSELLING

1 **Your aim is to teach the truth to someone who does not know or understand what God has done for him in Christ, or to bring the Word of the Lord that will penetrate to the heart in the situation of need.**

2 **You aim is to help the person hear what God is saying to him in that situation; but he has to believe what God says and act on His Word. You are not helping him to find alternatives to faith and obedience.**

3 **You stand with a believer against any way in which he has allowed the enemy to put him into bondage;** but you do not do the deliverance for him without the necessary repentance and co-operation on his part. He has to exercise authority over the enemy, or the deliverance will only be short-lived.

4 **You do not take the person into the past, but into the Truth of God's Word, into what He has done for him in Christ.** It is this Truth that will set him free as he hears it, believes it and acts upon it.

5 **If necessary you help him to see that he needs to forgive** and not drag the weight of the past into his walk with Jesus.

6 **You are not to be used as a substitute for faith in God.** Prayer with you is not an alternative to walking in the truth as a disciple of Jesus.

7 **Allow the Word to do the work!** You will be amazed at the liberating power of the Gospel!

8 **Your sensitivity to the Spirit will help the person to see clearly the issues he cannot see for himself** because of the confusion that has resulted from trying to find his own solutions to his problems.

THE BENEFITS

It is rewarding to see that the time devoted to a person in this way, not only brings the liberty promised in scripture, but **you see him being built up in faith so that he will be able to withstand future trials,** and that he grows in his knowledge in such a way that he becomes an ambassador of the Truth to others.

> I pray that you may be active in sharing your faith, so that you will have a full understanding of every good thing we have in Christ (Philem. v. 6).

It is rewarding to see a person being fruitful for the Kingdom of God, instead of feeling he is held back by the weight he has been dragging along because of his wrong self-image. It is encouraging to see a person rise up in faith and authority to overcome the enemy. It causes your heart to rejoice to see someone who was problem-centred become purpose-orientated, on fire with love for God and desiring above all else to do His will, instead of seeing himself as a problem, a failure, a nuisance.

What a difference between the new, assured of his place in Christ and of the Father's love for him, and the old, bound by fear and introspection!

This is not to say that he will have no further difficulties and challenges to face; but **he is now equipped to face whatever the future might bring because of his faith in God and His Word.**

> But thanks be to God, who always leads us in triumphal procession in Christ and through us spreads everywhere the fragrance of the knowledge of him (2 Cor. 2:14).

Also he has now discovered to whom to turn in future times of crisis. **He has direct access to God through Jesus Christ.** With a sincere heart and full assurance of faith he can come into the Holy of Holies. He is learning how to pray things through with

God, to hear Him for himself, **to be Counsellor-led, not counsellor-dependent!**

Of course you have only helped him to establish a process that will need to continue for the rest of his life. But you have done what is asked of you by the Lord: to make disciples. You have not made his decisions for him, nor sought to lord it over him. You have taught him what it is to be a responsible disciple. And it will not be long before he disciples others, for now he has a grasp of the Truth that he knows will set others free.

The believer's spirit is sanctified and now the process of sanctifying his soul is taking place. Jesus prayed for His disciples: 'Sanctify them by the truth; your word is truth' (John 17:17).

Any believer is in good hands because the Lord Himself will sanctify him through and through, spirit, soul and body (1 Thess. 5:23). His purpose as a Christian is to live the life of the Kingdom God has placed within him. The measure he gives will be the measure he receives. **In the past he sowed into the Truth sparingly and reaped sparingly; now he can sow generously and reap generously** (2 Cor. 9:6).

He has learnt that he will not receive from God on his own terms, but on those the Lord lays down in His Word. **It is for him as a believer to believe, as a disciple to submit himself to God, as a child of the Kingdom to give cheerfully.** And he knows that:

God is able to make all grace abound to you, so that in all things at all times, having all that you need, you will abound in every good work (2 Cor. 9:8).

He can believe the promise:

You will be made rich in every way so that you can be generous on every occasion (2 Cor. 9:11).

Instead of the former self-pitying, poverty mentality, he can believe in the rich inheritance he has in Christ.

And all this is the work of God's grace! He will be eternally grateful for the love and mercy shown him by Jesus. **He will not easily set aside the grace of God,** for he will not want to return to the bondage to self he was in before he saw the need to 'lose' himself. He will not want to return to law once he has tasted the rewards of faith.

He has been liberated from Satan's grasp by his own grasp of the Truth and can exercise his God-given authority over the enemy.

So if the Son sets you free, you will be free indeed (John 8:36).

The Son has indeed set him free, and if he is wise he will heed the warnings of scripture not to return to a life of bondage:

I run in the path of your commands, for you have set my heart free (Ps. 119:32).

And so now he can truly be led in triumph. He is free because the Lord has set him free. He is learning to walk in the Spirit and experience freedom in every area of his life, which he yields to the sovereignty of the Holy Spirit.

No longer does he need to fear the spirits that are at work in the world, for:

You, dear children, are from God and have overcome them, because the one who is in you is greater than the one who is in the world (1 John 4:4).

He has the faith to overcome the world:

For everyone born of God overcomes the world. This is the victory that has overcome the world, even our faith. Who is it that overcomes the world? Only he who believes that Jesus is the Son of God (1 John 5:4–5).

And he knows an eternal inheritance awaits him:

> To him who overcomes, I will give the right to sit with me on
> my throne, just as I overcame and sat down with my Father
> on his throne (Rev. 3:21).

Like Paul there is a cry of joy and victory in his heart. **He has
victory over the past and the confusion he has experienced for so
long.** Now he does not need to fear the future, not even death:

> The sting of death is sin, and the power of sin is the law. But
> thanks be to God! He gives us the victory through our Lord
> Jesus Christ (1 Cor. 15:56–7).

Now he can set his heart on obeying the apostle's exhortation:

> Therefore, my dear brothers, **stand firm. Let nothing move
> you.** Always give yourselves fully to the work of the Lord,
> because you know that your labour in the Lord is not in
> vain (v. 58).

He is not only on the defensive; he now wants to influence
others with the Truth that they too might be set free. He is
no longer the enemy's punch bag, but is able to overcome
him:

> **You give me your shield of victory, and your right hand
> sustains me; you stoop down to make me great . . . You
> armed me with strength for battle; you made my adversaries
> bow at my feet. You made my enemies turn their backs in
> flight, and I destroyed my foes** (Ps. 18:35, 39–40).

Of course he will need to guard against pride and a return to
self-sufficiency. His soul will rise up above the Spirit if allowed
the opportunity!

Be on your guard; stand firm in the faith; be men of courage; be strong (1 Cor. 16:13).

He finds his strength in the truth of Jesus Christ and will do well to remember that apart from Him he can do nothing!

You may lose sight of the one you have helped. You may continue in a relationship of mutual encouragement. In either case you can give him the advice Paul gave Timothy:

But as for you, continue in what you have learned and have become convinced of, because you know those from whom you learned it (2 Tim. 3:14).

Each of us has to learn to:

Throw off everything that hinders and the sin that so easily entangles, and let us run with perseverance the race marked out for us (Heb. 12:1).

We are constantly reaching out for what lies ahead of us, taking hold of everything for which Christ Jesus has taken hold of us. And we can be confident that:

He will keep you strong to the end, so that you will be blameless on the day of our Lord Jesus Christ (1 Cor. 1:8).

And when difficulties arise instead of being miserable or despondent, we can afford to be confident:

Being confident of this, that he who began a good work in you will carry it on to completion until the day of Christ Jesus (Phil. 1:6).

And we won't let the devil or anyone else tell us otherwise!

Further Study

For further reading:

Victory over the Darkness (Monarch Publications)	Neil Anderson
The Bondage Breaker (Monarch Publications)	Neil Anderson
In Christ Jesus (Hodder & Stoughton)	Colin Urquhart
Personal Victory (Hodder & Stoughton)	Colin Urquhart
Listen and Live (Hodder & Stoughton)	Colin Urquhart
Anything You Ask (Hodder & Stoughton)	Colin Urquhart
Receive Your Healing (Hodder & Stoughton)	Colin Urquhart
Thriving on the Truth (New Wine)	Dan Chesney
Toxic Love (Pillar Books)	Malcolm Smith
Forgiveness (Pillar Books)	Malcolm Smith

All the above are available from:
    Kingdom Faith Ministries
    Roffey Place, Old Crawley Road
    Faygate, Horsham, West Sussex,
    RH12 4SA

The following audio cassette series are also available:
BREAKTHROUGH:
by Colin Urquhart
    A series of four cassettes about overcoming the enemy

BREAKING BONDAGES:
by Dan Chesney
    Breaking repetitive behaviours
    Dealing with thoughts and emotions
    Winning over crises and anger
    Living what we are

DIRECT COUNSELLING:
by Colin Urquhart
    Twelve cassettes from a Conference covering the areas of
    teaching given in this book; how to counsel with the Truth